FINDING MERCY
IN THIS WORLD

A Memoir

Catherine Johnson

ENDICOTT
and HUGH
BOOKS

Copyright © 2018 by Catherine Johnson

All rights reserved.

This story is based on actual people and events. It relies on the author's memory and imagination for some of its scenes and dialogue.

"The Sound of Grace" is excerpted from "The Sound of Grace," first published in Face to Face (Linda Hogan and Brenda Peterson, editors) Copyright © 2004, North Point Press, a division of Farrar, Straus and Giroux.

ISBN: 978-0-9993646-0-4 Trade paperback

Published in the United States
Endicott and Hugh Books
PO Box 13305
Burton, WA

All rights reserved, including the right to reproduce this book, or portions thereof, in any form. Published by Endicott and Hugh Books, Burton, Washington. www.endicottandhughbooks.com

Printed in the United States of America
Cover photograph by Catherine Johnson

Book design by Novak Creative, Inc.

For Dana, Kate, and Alex

PROLOGUE

For 1500 years, people have been making this pilgrimage.
Our footsteps follow theirs, just as others will one day follow ours.
In the solitude I hear them, feel them moving all around me. It is as if
I have entered an invisible, timeless, ever-flowing river of souls. There
have been so many moments walking, when I was sure I heard someone
coming up behind me, but when I turned to look, found no one there.
Perhaps though, it is the eternal One who is everywhere,
and all the seekers that ever were or will be, including me,
are simply part of that great Mystery.
(Journal entry: April 17, 2015, Camino de Santiago, Spain)

A number of years ago during a faculty lunch, a colleague quipped, "There are two questions and one spark that ignite the fire of spiritual seeking. 'Does God Exist? And, does He know my name?'"

"And the spark?" I asked.

"Loss," he said. Then, in a softer voice of one who has known its pain, "A loss big enough that it rends the fabric of your life, so that all you thought you knew is shredded by the tear."

Mine is not a remarkable story although it seems a miracle to me. Mine is a story of a profound loss and the long search for forgiveness. It is also a love story: love of the natural world, love of women, love of family and community.

As I enter my sixty-third year, I can see that I have always been walking in that river of souls, looking for God and God's forgiveness, but it was my own forgiveness I needed most. And although I couldn't hear her footsteps, God was always there, walking with me. This is the story of that journey: a journey I could not have made alone, a journey that binds me to all of humankind and a journey that is not yet over. This is my story.

PART I

BEFORE

It was the summer of 1969, I was 14 years old and had finally graduated: from camper to counselor, from girl to young woman, from small musings to bigger dreams.

"Do you ever think about leaving Indiana?" I asked my friend Rita, as we lay on our backs rocking gently atop an enormous load of freshly baled hay. Beneath us the old flatbed truck labored up a dusty road; above us a canvas of afternoon sky stretched tautly, perfect in its bright July blue.

With her eyes closed and a long stem of grass between her teeth, Rita considered my question. We were the same age. She was tall like me, had an oval face framed by straight blonde hair held in place with a red bandanna. Her sunburned skin, dusty overalls, and faded chambray shirt made her seem as though she was made of summer. Rita turned onto her side and looked at me.

"Where would you go?" she asked.

"I don't know, California. Montana. Some place really different."

"Hmm, never really thought about it."

With that she lay back, closed her eyes, and continued chewing on her stem of dry alfalfa. Beneath us the truck lurched and shifted into a lower gear; I could hear gravel grind under the tires as the engine groaned.

"Geez us, I hope we make it up the hill," I said.

"We'll make it. Becky's driving."

If Rita ever worried about things, I never saw it. She seemed to take disappointment in stride and find contentment in small things.

"So you don't wonder what it would be like to live somewhere else, different sights, different trees?"

"Nope," she answered, then as if reconsidering: "I don't know, maybe. Becky is talking about moving to Florida to work with race horses." Rita paused, turned her head slightly, and opened one eye to see if I was listening. "I don't think Becky would go just for different trees."

Playfully, I punched Rita in the shoulder. "Fuck you." Then I too lay back and watched the sky.

Rita often made me smile. She had a slow way of speaking and a kind of droll humor; she could turn an ordinary conversation somehow funny.

The truck made it up the last hill and turned into the entrance of the summer camp where we worked. Becky shouted up from the truck's cab.

"Hey! One of you get the gate."

Becky was Rita's older sister. At 18, she was a senior counselor, in charge of the horse barn, and Rita and I had been assigned to her tutelage. From Becky we would learn to muck out stalls, clean hooves, comb out manes, and curry coats, as well as saddle and bridle and ride "drag," or last, behind the campers on their trail rides.

"I'll get the gate," Rita said, sitting up and scooting towards the end of the hay bales. As she disappeared off the back of the truck, I took in the view.

Of the two summer camp properties owned by the Archdiocese of Indianapolis and situated in the rolling hill country of south-central Indiana, Camp Christina was the less developed. It was little more than a handful of surplus army tents tentatively pitched on a bald hilltop of rough, dry grass—grass that often went too long uncut and gave the place a slightly shabby appearance. To parents accustomed to sophisticated or expensive summer camp environments, Camp Christina looked more like a MASH unit. But to the campers who went there, and the staff who worked there, Christina was a beloved landscape.

From Christina's open summit, steep wooded ridges and ravines fell away to the valleys below, like folds in a great green robe. A small brown water pond served as a swimming lake and a covered pavilion offered the only protection when afternoon storms rolled out of the west, darkening the sky and threatening to tear the tents from their stakes. From the highest point, where the campfire circle lay, we could gaze out across a wide valley dotted with the patchwork fields of tiny farming communities. Those communities included pockets of Amish and Mennonite farmers in their broad-brimmed hats and horse-drawn buggies, as well as the gas pump and general store towns with names like: Stonehead, Story, and Needmore, whose population in 1969 stood at only 11. "No wonder they need more," was a standard camp joke.

The land that surrounded Camp Christina was rural, the pace of life slow, the woods still a little wild. Perhaps that is what bound us girls to camp and each other, that little bit of wildness. When we were at camp, we ran for the joy of speed, slept outside on hard ground, got soaked in the rain, and dried ourselves by smoky fires. In that sisterhood, we got dirty, worked hard, and played with silly and reckless abandon. Maybe that's why we faithfully returned each summer, to reclaim our wildness, the one that our parents, the Catholic Church, and society at large sought so hard to tame.

Becky parked the hay truck in front of the barn while the horses grazed lazily out back. Soon we could hear their heavy bodies wandering along the barn wall, snorting and heaving. Road Runner, a small dark gelding with a bad sway back, peeked at the corner and whinnied loudly.

"Hey, boy." Rita walked over and offered him a small handful of fresh hay. He chomped it greedily from her palm.

"Don't be temptin' him," Becky said. "He'll just want more. C'mon now, let's go. We got a lot to unload before the dinner bell rings."

On first glance, Rita appeared like a taller and lankier version of her older sister. Both had long blonde hair and fair skin, faces that were open and expressive, blue eyes that got lost in the tight squint of their smiles. But where Rita was easily content, Becky was thoughtful and determined. And where Rita was long, Becky was round, really round. One of the first things I learned about her was that she could float vertically in the water, like a cork. Whenever Becky went swimming, the littler campers were on her immediately, clambering over her like a bobbing jungle gym, seeing if they could submerge her. It was not easy to do. Becky also had a strong will and a sense of her own direction. She never imposed that will on others, but stayed true to her own compass. She was stronger than any woman I had ever met and moved with extraordinary grace for someone so large. She was the only woman I knew who rode a motorcycle, smoked a pipe, and seemed absolutely sure of herself. At 14, if I wanted to be like anyone, it was Becky.

"Uh oh," Rita said in a confidential tone while rubbing Road Runner's nose, "the boss has spoken." She gave the horse a playful rub on his forehead and turned to me as if I was the one holding up the show. "Well, you heard Becky, let's go."

The three of us started in. Becky and Rita stood up in the hayloft above the stalls; I stood on the back of the truck lifting bales to them. Becky snagged each 40-pound bale that I struggled to lift with her hay hook and tossed it like it was nothing to Rita, who stacked it against the far wall.

While we worked, the two sisters teased each other playfully and joined together to poke fun at me, especially as I attempted to match their work ethic, their endurance, and their strength. While I was tall and strong, in photographs my nearly 6-foot frame stands a head above almost everyone else, I was not accustomed to hard physical work.

My mother and father were from wealthy families and had inherited the means, advantages, and attitudes that come from such beginnings. Determined to give me everything, I, their only child, grew up with unlimited opportunities and ample allowances. Becky and Rita, on the other hand, came from a hard-working, blue-collar family. They expected nothing and knew they would have to work for the things they wanted. One of the many lessons I took away from those early years at camp was an appreciation for manual labor, a respect for those whose lives were bound to it, and an understanding that my race and class ensured that I could choose such work, or not.

On that particular afternoon, I was a willing although flagging assistant. Every time I stopped, Becky and Rita seemed to get a second wind and speed up.

"C'mon, Johnson, you restin' again?" they would yell from the loft above.

Reluctantly, I would lift another bale, the twine biting into my hands, my arms burning and my legs growing rubbery with the effort. Above us, the late afternoon heat seared the galvanized roof, raising the temperature in the dusty barn to an almost unbearable level. The rafters creaked and popped loudly, as the wood expanded. We were sweating out more than we could return to our bodies, even though we swallowed long draws of water from a glass gallon jar that we refilled on the hour from a rusty spigot outside the tack room.

After 3 hours of unloading hay bales I was whipped, my head hurt, and I needed a break. Sitting down, I silently declared a strike. Immediately, Becky and Rita started in on me. I refused to respond and simply lay back on the hay with my eyes closed, feigning heat exhaustion. No matter what they said, I did not respond.

It felt wonderful to stop; I listened as the blood pounding in my head eased, the insects buzzed, and Becky and Rita conferred in low voices. Then one of them started climbing down the ladder. I knew by the voice that it was Becky, coming to drag me to my feet.

"C'mon, Johnson," she said.

I opened my eyes a little. Becky stood over me extending a hand. Her face was flushed and dirt streaked, her brow knitted with just the tiniest hint of concern. I reached for her hand. Our palms fit easily together, damp, hot, and gritty. A different kind of heat flared as I held onto her hand. My breath paused and my heart raced. What couldn't have lasted more than a second, seemed to stretch on: our eyes meeting and hands touching. My whole body buzzed.

Had Becky been a boy it would have all been so much clearer, but she was not. Becky was a girl, like me. At 14, growing up in Indiana, I had no word to name what it was I felt. So, I did the only thing I could think of to do. I pulled on her hand as hard as I could, pitching her forward onto the hay next to me. A wrestling match ensued. It only took a minute before Rita jumped down and joined in too. When one of us would pin the other down, the third would pull off whoever was on top, keeping the game going. Barn dust covered our arms and faces while the raw smells of earth, alfalfa, leather, and horse surrounded us. We stuffed hay down each other's shirts and tickled one another 'til we couldn't breathe. And although I begged for mercy a hundred times, I hoped the game would never end. Eventually though, Becky must have felt the weight of her responsibility.

"Alright, God dammit." She stood up and brushed herself off. "We've got a lot of hay still to unload. It's only an hour until dinner and the truck has to be empty, ready to go first thing in the morning."

Rita and I sat back on our heels, still breathing heavy. Becky stood in front of us with her hands on her hips, attempting to appear stern. Her attempt, so poorly executed, caused Rita and me to collapse into one another again laughing hysterically.

"C'mon," Becky reasoned. "Father Schneider will be royally pissed off, if this truck isn't unloaded by morning." Seeing that we were unfazed by her concerns, she resorted to bribery. "I'll buy you beer on Saturday night."

This got our attention.

"A six-pack?"

"No, just some beer."

"Uh-uh, gotta be a six," Rita and I chorused together, arms crossed over our chests.

"OK," Becky relented. "A six."

Rita hopped to her feet and slapped my hand as she walked by. Becky gave me a playful shove and climbed back up into the loft. I grabbed a bale of hay and lifted it with new energy.

Although Becky had been determined to stack the hay by dinner, she had misjudged the effects of the heat, the quality of her help, and the task itself. We were still hard at work when the dinner bell rang and had only just finished when the bell rang again for evening campfire. The loft was finally filled and the leftover bales stacked like a great staircase at the far end of the barn. As Becky and Rita jumped from the last onto the floor, I met them. "We did it, we're done!"

All the way out the front pasture, we continued to congratulate ourselves and replay some of the events of the day. But, as we closed the pasture gate behind us and headed up the road to the main part of camp, we grew quiet.

A band of pale pink light stretched barely visible in the west and the sky overhead was turning into night. The air was deathly still, humid and hot, and we were bone tired and filthy from the work. A star appeared as we passed the lake and a chorus of frogs greeted us.

The words were out of my mouth before the thought had formed fully in my mind. "Last one in…" I slapped Rita on the arm, Becky on the shoulder, and took off at a dead run. The small lake waited like a cool dark mirror. As I hit the dock I slowed, just enough to untie my boots and kick them off. Rita caught up with Becky and both were only steps behind. When I remember us that night, we are, all three, leaping free of anything that might hold us: rising high into the day's last light, knees pulled tight to our chests, laughing and falling, three perfect cannonballs shattering the lake's still surface. In my imagination I see the last drops of our collective splash raining down like silver sparks upon us.

Later that night the air was sultry and sleep would not come. I lay on my cot, on top of my sleeping bag, and listened to the small murmurs and dream rustling of the campers in my tent. I thought about the day's events and my friends, Becky and Rita. I felt so at home with them, so easy. And yet with Becky there was something more. Eventually, a little breeze rose and came gliding across the hilltop, cooling the air and quieting the camp. Grateful for the cooler air, but still unable to sleep, I stepped into my jeans and slipped from the tent.

As a senior counselor, Becky had a tent of her own. I walked over to it and stood outside, listening. Becky's breath moved in a regular rhythm punctuated occasionally by a soft snore. I wanted to go in, to be near her. The longer I stood there, the louder my heart beat. There was a hunger in me that I had never felt, to be near another, to feel their warmth and the softness of their skin. But, I knew that what I wanted was somehow wrong. So, I rested my forehead against the tent, feeling the rough fabric against my face. Squeezing my eyes shut, I tried to hold back hot tears. They came anyway, sliding down my cheeks.

Just hours before, I had felt so happy; now I felt frustrated and confused. Wiping away my tears, I walked. My steps took me out to campfire circle. There were still a few embers glowing. I stirred them and watched the sparks float upward like an offering or a prayer. Below, the valley lay sealed in fog. It looked as if you could step off the hilltop and walk. I wished I could.

I must have decided that night that I would not risk my friendship with Becky, because, although my crush on her lasted the rest of that summer and a shadow of it remained for years, I never told her.

It would be many years before I would come out as a lesbian and many more after that, before I would fall completely in love, and feel again such innocent wonder and desire. Still, I had cracked the door of my sexuality and peeked in. It was a door I could close, but one that would not stay locked.

Outward Bound

Two years later, I found myself on a Greyhound bus bound for Duluth, Minnesota. It was early evening. The rain was falling steadily and the temperature dropping quickly. It felt more like early spring than midsummer and the bus felt drafty and cold. I pulled on my sweater and my wool cap. Oh great, I thought, I'm already wearing everything warm that I brought and I am not even outside yet.

I had chosen to sit alone although there were a number of others on the bus heading for the Minnesota Outward Bound School. We were obvious in our brand new leather boots, work pants with the creases still ironed in, and flannel shirts that looked stiff rather than soft. We were a bunch of city kids heading into the woods for a month who looked too clean, too pressed, and too country club for the clothes we were wearing. I sat alone so I wouldn't have to talk to anyone. While I could be very conversant if asked, I was often at a loss for how to begin. Ever since entering high school, I had been learning about my social shortcomings and self-doubts. Two girls across the aisle smacked their gum, talked loudly, and giggled in high-pitched voices. Why did everyone else seem so cool? I turned my face to the window and stared into the gathering darkness.

Traveling northward, the towns became smaller and the forested stretches of highway in between, longer. The weather, the darkness, and the warm yellow glow from the occasional houses we passed worked on me. I started to feel lonely and wondered why I had wanted to do this in the first place.

It was Fitz's idea. I remembered a conversation that my friend Mary Fitzgerald and I had had the previous summer. Mary had just returned from her Outward Bound course in Minnesota. We were at camp, sitting on the porch railing outside the canteen, sipping sodas. Mary was lobbying me.

"Cath, you should go. You would love it."

"Why would I want to go, mosquitoes as big as the mess tent, carrying a canoe…"

"Portaging," Mary corrected.

"Right, portaging a canoe on my shoulders for miles through the woods. Mary, those things weigh a ton."

"Yah, but you get stronger, Cath, and carrying them gets easier."

I had to admit Mary looked great after her month-long course. Tan and muscled, she could out-swim and out-hike me and everyone else by a mile. She also had learned how to lash, how to read a map, and use a compass. She had learned first aid and how to leave a campsite as if you'd never been there. Mary excitedly shared her new skills with me and with the campers as well, and that summer the "camp-craft" activity truly changed. We stopped making coal gardens from ammonia and charcoal briquettes; we stopped tracing leaves on construction paper. Instead we started making shelters from downed wood and sleeping out beneath them, fixing our breakfasts over a campfire, foraging for edible plants, and learning to track. That was the summer we started really living outdoors, all because Mary had gone to Outward Bound.

"Cath, you just have to do it."

Hopping down off the railing and putting my Mountain Dew bottle in the empties flat, I said, "Fitz, you are crazy. You will never catch me doing anything like that."

I should have known, though, the idea would seed itself in me, would stay with me all fall. There were other changes in Mary that I noticed. She seemed more confident and sure of herself and she talked more and more about camping trips she wanted to take. If Becky's sister Rita wasn't interested in traveling west, Mary Fitzgerald was completely up for it. And, she was convinced that if we, we being the operative pronoun, were going to travel there, I would need the skills that Outward Bound taught. Eventually, I came to believe that too and now here I was in northern Minnesota, headed for my Outward Bound course.

"Duhh– looth. This 's Duhh-looth."

I opened my eyes to the driver's announcement and to the bright lights of the Duluth bus station. Other kids were stretching and rubbing sleep from their faces as well. I looked at my watch; it was 8:00 PM. One by one we grabbed our duffels and dragged them into the depot.

Once inside we were greeted by the Outward Bound staff. Unlike us, they looked completely at home in their clothes: wool sweaters that had been darned with different colored threads, wool socks that bagged 'round the ankles, and sneakers that were well worn, some held together with athletic tape. And although the temperature was barely above 50 degrees, all of them were wearing shorts. One of the first things I noticed was that these people were a hairy lot; many of the men had scraggly beards and the women clearly did not shave their legs. I was both attracted to what I saw and uncomfortable with it as well. I could tell that these women and men were at home in their skin, like I felt at camp, yet their wild look was a more extreme version than any I had so far known.

Quickly a guy named Bucky who wore his baseball cap backwards divided us into groups, or "brigades" as we learned to call ourselves. I dragged my duffel over and stood with eight other young women, all of us between the ages of 16 and 19. A tall but spare young man approached us. He was slightly bow-legged, wearing the slouching wool socks, worn sneakers, shorts, and heavy wool sweater of his tribe. His hair was long, salt and pepper gray, pulled back in a ponytail. There was something odd about him though, something that caught my attention. When he spoke I figured it out. He wasn't a he at all; he was a she.

"I'm Rita Pougiales, one of your instructors."

Rita P. was lean and muscled, soft-voiced with kind brown eyes. She had no need for a bra; by the end of the 28 days, neither would I. Weight loss and a chest wall muscled hard from paddling every day leaves a girl pretty flat. Rita P. also had more body hair than any woman I had ever met. Often during that first week of the course I would look at her, still not quite believing she was a woman. I had only left home that morning but I had traveled a world away.

"We'll be a mobile brigade," Rita explained. "That means we won't be going to base camp until the very end of the course." She paused before finishing. "This way we'll be able to travel further into the Quetico wilderness."

The last part sounded a little like a sell job, a way of rationalizing a more challenging trip. It was the pause that gave it away.

"You'll need to pull out what you will carry for the next 28 days; the rest will go to base camp and be returned to you at the end of the course."

I looked at the others; thankfully they too seemed perplexed by Rita P.'s instructions. The clothing list sent by Outward Bound had been for a 28-day course. What was I supposed to leave behind? Rita must have read my mind; she stepped over someone digging into her duffel and came over to me.

"Hi, Rita Pougiales." She extended her hand.

"Cathy Johnson," I said, accepting it. We stood eye to eye. I didn't often meet women who were as tall as me. "So, what should I take out?"

"One pair of pants, two pairs of shorts, a couple of T-shirts, one long-sleeved shirt, your wool jacket and hat, four pairs of socks."

Four pairs of socks, now I knew what really mattered—socks.

"Bring your tennis shoes, bathing suit, a couple of bandannas, one can be your towel."

My towel? I tried to imagine drying my body with a handkerchief. "Only one pair of pants?"

"You'll only wear them at night." Rita smiled and laid her hand on my shoulder. Was I supposed to be reassured? Then she stepped on to inspect someone else's pile. Years later Rita Pougiales would show up again in my life, serving as my faculty advisor during the last year of my undergraduate degree. Over the years I have come to think of her as one of the way-showers in my life, one of the people who appeared at an important moment and pointed me in a direction, simply by being themselves.

Having culled from our clothes the few things we would actually carry, the nine of us gave up our duffels and piled into a Ford van, which Rita drove another hour into the north woods. Finally we arrived, but to where? Clambering out of the van, we stood beside it in the absolute silent darkness.

"Wait here," Rita said and disappeared into the brush. All of us had flashlights but no one thought to get hers out. Maybe we were in shock. The forest was everywhere—close. If all the trees had taken a step forward, the road and all of us would have simply disappeared.

A light rain still fell and the chill seemed to creep from the ground up. I took a deep breath and smelled the pungent scent of evergreen and the sweet decay of moist earth. Momentarily Rita reappeared with our second instructor, a woman named Marty. Where Rita was long and lanky, Marty was short and powerfully built. Our group followed them a few hundred yards into the woods, where we found a large tarp pitched along with four tents. Marty had set up the camp and prepared hot chocolate for our arrival. And although we were tired from our various travels, we dutifully sat in a circle, beneath the tarp with the mist dripping from its corners, and introduced ourselves. As we sipped hot chocolate, we said our name and where we were from. Not one name would be remembered come morning, but we participated in the exercise anyway. Then we were off to bed, to cold nylon sleeping bags. I remember, though, that I was so tired it felt like heaven to simply lie down. Had I known that I would experience this same sentiment every night for the next 27, I might have left right then.

I was the youngest member of our brigade, having just 3 months before turned 16. I was also the most physically fit, which, looking back, was not saying much. The next morning we had to carry, to portage, our gear and food 2 miles to the edge of a lake where the canoes were waiting. We were paired up and given a large canvas pack, a Duluth Pack, in which to put our clothes, sleeping bags, and a few miscellaneous items of group gear such as a tent, first aid kit, pots and pans, shovel, or tarp. Once the gear was equally divided and our packs packed, we had to decide who would carry the other items. Along with our personal packs, there were canoe paddles and life jackets to be portaged, as well as three large food packs. The food packs were the same cavernous Duluth model, but stuffed to seam-splitting capacity. There was food enough in each for a week. This was long before freeze-dried meals and energy bars. These packs contained bags of oatmeal, tins of sardines, tubs of peanut butter, blocks of cheese. The food packs were meant to last until our first re-supply. The lunch pack seemed particularly onerous. I eyed it warily, having a hunch it would end up on my back.

Rita started lifting packs onto shoulders while Marty handed out other pieces of gear. When Rita went to hoist the lunch pack, it was clear just what a monster it really was; she lifted it a few inches, took a step, and then set it back down with a thud. Then she looked in my direction. I knew it.

"Cathy." She motioned for me to come over.

I was not surprised, and truthfully I felt proud that I could be of service in this way. I stepped over and faced the lunch pack.

"I think you better turn around."

"What?"

"Turn around and sit down. I'll help you get into the straps and then help you stand up."

I stopped feeling proud and started feeling scared as I slid my arms into the unpadded leather straps. Rita stood in front of me.

"I will pull you forward, you get your weight over your feet." Rita braced her feet against mine and hauled. I struggled to get my legs under me.

"Fuck!" I forgot my manners as I gasped for air upon reaching vertical. Someone in the group said: "Whoa, way to go."

Rita smiled as she handed me two canoe paddles to lean on for balance. "When you need to rest, lean back against a tree, then bend your knees a little; some of the weight will be taken by the tree." She demonstrated. "Or, you can bend over and let the paddles take the weight." She demonstrated this too: pushing the paddles out at a 40-degree angle with their handles hitting just below the top of the pack. "The way skiers catch their breath by leaning their shoulders on their poles." Once again she laid a less than reassuring hand on my shoulder. "You can do it, just take it slow, don't hurry."

It was the longest 2 miles I would ever walk and in the years to come, whenever I shouldered a heavy load or faced a demanding physical task, I would remember that first morning at Outward Bound.

Mary had been right: as the course progressed we all got stronger, more confident, and more capable. We learned to paddle on flat water and white, through storms and stiff winds. We learned to rock climb, navigate, and cook good food in a single pot. We also learned to get along. Everyone has idiosyncrasies. Some we learned to live with, while others we had to work out. Since we were literally relying on each other, we had to get along. Carol, the oldest in our group at 19, had an especially annoying habit of snatching the map out of my hand when I took too long to determine our position. One day when she grabbed it, I grabbed it back.

"Listen Carol, when you're navigating I give you all the time in the world. I want the same from you when it's my turn." Carol looked stunned. People rarely see me angry, so when they do, they can't help but be surprised and often a little intimidated.

"OK! Shit. Read the map then."

Forty-five minutes later we were still looking for our portage. I was trying to match the shoreline of the lake with that on the map without success. Our canoes were rafted up with everyone waiting—waiting on me. Carol reached across to take the map. "Uh-uh." I wagged my finger back and forth. "It's my turn."

Her face tightened and she took a deep breath, let it go, and returned to waiting. After a few more moments I gave up: "You are really way better at this than me. Maybe you better look." I handed Carol the map. Quickly, she figured out where we were and off we went. She and I reached a truce of some sort that day. When it was my turn to navigate she would be more patient and I would ask for her help sooner. By the end of the course, we had become friends.

Slowly but surely the weeks passed. I grew to love the call of the loons eerily echoing out across the lake. Every now and then we'd hear a wolf howl or owls calling. The night sounds in that country seemed magical to me. I began to feel more and more at home, getting lost in the daily rhythm of the draw and feather, reach and dip of my paddle. It was a motion repeated over and over again, across miles and miles of iron-colored water. Hadn't I always done this? We were often up before the sun, and still paddling as it went down. The long hours also came to feel familiar. The mosquitoes were, at times, ferocious but I learned to live with them too. Everything seemed to be as it should be.

Outward Bound had helped me find something I was really good at, naturally good at—wilderness travel. School did not come easy for me. I spent more time in the gym than the library. Even when I applied myself, I only made average grades. Attending a private girls school run by the Sisters of Providence, my classmates were either headed for the convent or for universities known for their academic rigor, places such as MIT, Notre Dame, or Georgetown. Even though I had only finished my sophomore year, I had pretty much decided I was not college material and I certainly was not going to become a nun. I liked to drink, do my own thing, and say "fuck" way too much. So, having ruled out the only two options in my very narrow field of view, I was left with a huge question and its underlying anxiety: just what would I do with my life. Now, I had an idea. The freedom and self-reliance I felt at Outward Bound were unlike any I had known so far. This coupled with the natural beauty of the Boundary Waters and Quetico Provincial Parks made for an intoxicating experience: one that I felt determined to recreate in my life.

Since most of our brigade was off to college or soon to be, school was often the topic of evening conversation. Even our instructors were headed back to school, to a new college just opening in Washington State: a place called Evergreen. I listened with rapt attention as they talked about a school where you could get credit for mountain climbing, for studying wilderness instructing. By the end of the course, I was sure it would be the place for me in a couple of years. Me, who had been eyeing a future without college, now possessed an avid interest in going on. When I got home, my parents were stunned.

On the last night of the course, after we had eaten our fill of fresh food and rich dessert, and celebrated our journey together, I washed dishes beside Rita in the kitchen. I was proudly wearing my new dark green Minnesota Outward Bound T-shirt with a compass rose printed on the breast.

"Do you think I could ever be an instructor here?" I asked, trying to sound casual. I'm sure Rita could hear the longing in my voice.

"Sure," she answered without hesitation rinsing a plate and stacking it. "You're a natural leader, you just need to hone your skills, take as many trips as you can on your own, and when you're old enough, apply to instruct." I looked over at her. "Besides," she continued with a smile, "you don't shave your legs and you don't burn the oatmeal."

It was not a huge endorsement, but it was good enough. It was a star I could steer by, and for the next couple of years, I did.

THE ACCIDENT

Throughout high school, I returned to camp each summer. In my eyes, school was simply a necessary activity between camp and canoe trips in Minnesota. Being outdoors was what I lived for.

By June of 1973 the country stood deeply divided; the national mood was restless and dark. The United States was slogging through the final throes of its protracted mistake in Southeast Asia. Richard Nixon was facing serious allegations regarding his role in the Watergate break-in. The word *authority* had become suspect, too often synonymous with greed and deceit. Americans were losing faith in the institutions that had long sustained them: government, church, and family. Yet my small world seemed only lightly touched by this larger turmoil. Having just graduated from high school, I was full of optimism, confidence, and the sweet-blind arrogance of youth. I was now 18 years old and a senior counselor. Mary Fitzgerald and I had been hired that summer to teach the camp-craft program, together. And in the fall I planned to attend The Evergreen State College in Olympia, Washington. I was excited to leave home, to travel west, to grow up.

"You sure you can't come with us?" I asked Fitz as she was about to climb out of the Jeep. Somewhere in the distant suburban darkness a rooster crowed.

"No. Mom needs me to help around the house. What time is it anyway?"

"A little before 5."

"God, that was a long night."

The Arlington Drive-in Theater had a once a month, dusk to dawn billing. If you stayed through all four movies, you got free doughnuts and coffee, and the way Fitz and I saw it, the right to brag about the achievement.

"Mom knows we'll be off to camp at the end of the week," Fitz continued. "She's trying to get as much work out of me as she can before I go."

The light from a street lamp reflected off her wire-frame glasses. She yawned.

"I know," I said, catching her yawn. "My mom and dad wish I would stay home more too. Ever since graduation I have been either gone, or on the go."

"Well, what do you expect? You'll be at camp all summer and then you leave for college. You should have dinner, or something with them this week."

Fitz was right. My parents were quickly losing their only child to a life of her own. In the fall I would be going to school 2100 miles and a world away from Indianapolis, where I had grown up. They wanted nothing more than my happiness, but also must have felt the pain of my imminent departure. I decided Fitz's idea was a good one.

"I've got an idea," I said with enthusiasm. "You could spend the night on Wednesday. We'll have dinner with my folks and then leave for camp early on Thursday. If we leave really early, we can go to the gorge and do a little climbing."

"What about staff training? It's supposed to start at 5."

"That's what I mean; if we leave really early, we could climb and still get to camp on time."

"How early is early?"

"4:30?"

I gazed at Fitz with my most charming of looks, hoping to convince her. She was one of my best friends, the friend I counted on most for outdoor adventures.

"Cath, you're crazy. It's too much in one day. This trip today is nuts."

Fitz was referring to my plan to drop her off, pick up our friends Becky, Anita, and Claire, drive to Kentucky, and go caving.

"Aren't you tired?"

"Nope. I slept through most of the middle movie."

"Alfie"—we both sang out at the same time, our voices rising in a mocking chorus. Then we laughed.

Fitz climbed out of the Jeep, then stuck her head back in. "Call me when you get home. OK?"

"OK."

As I pulled away from Fitz's house, her porch light blinked off.

The streets of Indianapolis were quiet at that time of morning. I passed a few cars, a garbage truck, a couple of police cruisers idling side by side in a liquor store parking lot. The air had cooled the way it does before dawn. At a stoplight, I reached around on the back floor of the Jeep for my jean jacket. When I found it, I put it on and snapped it all the way up. Meanwhile, a turquoise Cadillac with a white leather top pulled up beside me. Even though the windows were rolled up, I could hear music pounding on the other side. When I looked over, the driver looked back at me. I tensed. Black man, white woman, empty street: a combination about which I had been taught to be wary. I tried to act nonchalant, turning my head back and keeping my gaze straight ahead, but I was listening hard for the slightest sound of a car door opening. Finally, the light changed. The tires on the big blue caddy squealed and burned, catapulting it through the intersection. I watched its taillights disappear and breathed a long sigh of relief.

At 18, I believed that I could do anything, be anyone I wanted. I liked thinking of myself as independent and invincible. The truth is I was often fearful, anything but certain, and definitely not invincible.

When I pulled up in front of the two-story brick house that belonged to Becky's family, the sky was just beginning to soften, the blackness of night giving way to the yellow-grayness of dawn. I hurried by the front porch of Becky's house and went quietly in the side door. Becky was at the kitchen table eating cold cereal.

"Hey," Becky said, sleepily nodding me to the chair across from her. I sat down and she pushed a box of Rice Krispies over to me.

"Bowls are in the dish rack," she added.

Feeling impatient, I wondered where Claire and Anita were; we had planned to leave at 5:30, it was already 5:45 AM. Becky must have seen me look at my watch.

"Relax, Johnson. We have plenty of time. Eat some cereal."

If Becky had flaws, I still couldn't see them. Even though the feelings I had for her at 14 had cooled, I still loved hanging out with her. When I was with Becky, I just felt at home. Now at 18, I was aware that this was true with many of my girl friends. With girls, I felt at home; but girls also turned my head, girls made my heart race, girls were whom I wanted to impress. It was girls, not boys, that I wanted to kiss. And, this realization scared the hell out of me.

Looking back, Becky probably would have been one of the easiest people to ask about my sexuality. But in Indianapolis, Indiana, in 1973, even asking the question seemed impossible.

"No thanks," I said, pushing the cereal box aside. "I had too many doughnuts and bad coffee with Fitz."

"You two do the dusk to dawn thing?"

"Uh-huh," I replied, crossing my arms over my chest and rocking proudly back in my chair. "It was really pretty silly. The movies were not that great either. *Bonnie and Clyde* played first."

"That's a good movie."

"Yah, but I've seen it before, three times. I'll tell you what the best movie was, the one playing in the car next to us. They made out, nonstop. He was all over her. For a while, Fitz and I wondered if they were going to do it right there next to us."

Becky laughed. "How come Fitz isn't coming with us?"

"Her mom is making her work around the house today."

Becky slid her chair back. "Did you two sleep at all?" Before I could answer, her younger sister, Claire, appeared in the kitchen wrestling her thick dark hair into a ponytail.

"'Morning, Claire," I said.

Our friend Anita, and Becky's other sister, Rita, spilled into the kitchen behind Claire.

"Johnsone." Anita greeted me, using her particular variation on my last name.

"Hey Anita. Hey Rita." I scooted my chair over to make more space at the table. Rita was still in her pajamas, but Anita, Becky, and Claire were dressed to go caving: army surplus pants, T-shirts, flannel shirts, and leather boots. We looked like an all-female ad for Red Wing Shoes.

Outside, the sky was beginning to lighten. Inside, the kitchen table was busy. Cereal box and milk jug moved back and forth across the table repeatedly while the volume of conversation was on the rise.

"Where are you guys going today?" Rita asked, sloshing the milk over the top of her too-full bowl of cereal. Without missing a beat,

Becky, the oldest, handed her sister a kitchen towel to sop up the spill.

"Mammoth cave," I answered, "in Kentucky."

Claire spoke up. "But we're not going where the tourists go—right?"

"Right. We are going to look for another cave that links up with Mammoth. And if we don't get going, we're never gonna get anywhere." Immediately, everyone stood up and started piling dishes in the sink.

"Can I come?"

Rita looked at Becky. Becky looked at me. I shrugged.

"I guess so, but it'll be crowded in the back." Rita headed up the stairs for her clothes. Becky made an extra cheese sandwich while Anita and Claire gathered up their things for the day. In a matter of minutes, we were hurrying out the front door. I was down the porch steps, when I heard Becky's mom.

"Are you all going in that?" She was pointing at my yellow Jeep parked alongside the curb. Standing in her doorway, Mrs. Ernstes clutched a thin cotton housecoat around a faded nightgown. Her large frame seemed barely covered by the paper-light material.

"Don't worry, Mom," Claire said over her shoulder. "We'll be back tonight."

As I climbed in the driver's side of the Jeep, I heard Mrs. Ernstes yell, "Rita, take this." While still holding her housecoat with one hand, she held out a blanket with the other. Rita ran back up the sidewalk to take the blanket from her mother. I have always wondered what words if any passed between the two, mother and daughter, meeting on their front porch. They could not have known it would be the last time.

At first we were a noisy group, flying down the interstate, shouting over one another, teasing each other while the wind flapped the Jeep's canvas top and the AM radio blared. But it was not long before the vibration of the road and the monotony of the drive worked its narcotic effect on the ones in back. With the blanket over them, they leaned against one another and fell silent, sleepy-eyed. Even Becky, riding in the front next to me, allowed her eyes to close. I switched off the radio and drove on in silence.

There was little traffic that morning. A bright orange ball of summer sun rose slowly from a field of green corn and I remember feeling something, something more than happiness. Today, I would name that feeling: blessed or graced. It was a brief moment when all of creation appeared as perfect. I could feel its beauty and pure peace: all about me, within me, and passing through me.

"Becky, check it out." I looked away from the fiery sunrise and found my good friend sound asleep. Her arms were crossed over her broad chest. I might have heard her snoring were it not for the wind flapping the Jeep's top. It thumped like a helicopter overhead. Glancing in the rearview mirror, I saw the others: Rita, Claire, and Anita. They too were sleeping soundly—curled in a tangled pile on the back floor, an orange and brown plaid blanket pulled over them. While the faces of Claire and Anita were slack and dream-softened, a slight smile lit Rita's, as if her playful nature refused to rest. I thought about her, how she was the one who always wanted to be included, who was always available for a water fight, a game of cards, any kind of harmless mischief or fun. As I gazed at the three of them sleeping, they looked very young.

Those moments return to me often. They come in my dreams and at odd times: when I am waiting for a light to change or when I am driving home late. A summer sunrise, the youthful faces of my sleeping friends: these are some of the things I remember about that morning, before my own eyes closed.

"Shit!" I said aloud, as my head jerked and my eyes snapped open, both seemingly at once. Not more than a couple of feet separated the front of the Jeep from the back end of a semi-truck. I could see a greasy handprint on the truck's door, a crack in one of its taillights, a ding in my own windshield, the speedometer reaching 80. The thought that we were about to slam into the back of that truck tore through me like lightning. I wrenched the steering wheel hard to the right and drove the brake pedal to the floor. The Jeep veered and the back end of the semi disappeared. A clear view of freshly plowed fields opened before me.

We're OK, I thought.

But even as I thought this, I knew it wasn't true. The left side tires lifted from the road, tilting the world. Then, for a few wild seconds we were sailing, suspended between fear and solid ground. Realizing what was about to happen, I whispered a desperate prayer, "Oh God."

The Jeep rolled: metal shrieked across the pavement, the top tore off, and the windshield shattered. Then came the blunt thud of impact. I remember something hitting me, or me hitting something, with a force that knocked me like a baseball out of the park. I remember landing, then nothing.

Later I would learn that I hit the steering wheel, severely fracturing my jaw. From the police report, I would learn that we rolled three times and traveled over 260 feet until a guardrail finally stopped us.

The Jeep came to a rest on its right side with the engine still running. Somehow Becky managed to unbuckle her seat belt and climb out. She must have helped me. We were standing on the shoulder of the interstate trying to orient ourselves, attempting to grasp what had happened, when Claire appeared, her thick brown hair a tangled mess, her face dirty and blouse torn.

"Rita's bad, Becky. She's real bad." Claire's voice came in a tight and frightened pitch: a younger sister looking to her older one for help.

Claire pointed behind us and Becky wheeled around to go, as did I, but I never took a step. Instead, I pitched forward and the pavement came up hard to meet me.

As I lay on the roadside, the world became a very small place. From the corner of my eye, I watched a fluorescent-green stream of antifreeze run towards me from the Jeep. I felt it pool beneath my shoulder and drench the back of my shirt. It was cold compared to the sticky-warm blood that soaked the right side of my face and neck. I knew that I was injured, but I had no idea how badly. Every now and then my body would shiver, launching rockets of pain in all directions. *Don't move*, I told myself, *just stay still*. I focused on the blue sky above and for a time I forgot about Becky, Rita, and the others. A chill crept up my limbs. Eventually it reached my center. The sky dimmed and everything slowed to a darkened stop.

I wish I had been braver that day, more helpful, but I was hurt and too afraid to move. When the Jeep rolled, the three in the back had been thrown out. Anita found herself sitting in the middle of the interstate while Claire landed in a freshly plowed field. Both were bruised and badly shaken, but otherwise unhurt. Rita had not been so lucky. She had been thrown against the guard railing headfirst. Years later Becky would tell me that she had tried to administer CPR to her dying sister that day, but had known the attempt was useless: with each compression of Rita's heart, more blood flowed from the wound on her head. I cannot imagine what it must have been like for Becky, to feel her sister slipping away as she tried to hold onto her.

Some minutes passed, I don't know how many. I don't know how long we waited for help to arrive, nor what happened when it finally did. It was as if someone had pushed the "pause" button in a video, and simply frozen the scene. And then, when the action resumed, all the sounds, smells, and feelings returned in an immediate rush. I was in the back of an ambulance, the siren wailing. Beside me a medic worked urgently on Rita. His back blocked my view of her, but beside his knee I recognized the orange and brown blanket that Rita's mother had sent along with us that morning. Now that same blanket was tangled in a sheet darkening with her daughter's blood.

The ambulance rushed us to a small town hospital. They wheeled Rita in first, then me. Bright lights, stainless steel, and green tile passed in a blur. A door closed behind us, and an orderly pulled a heavy canvas curtain between Rita and me. Immediately a nurse began cutting away my clothing. She started with my boots, then my pants. Meanwhile a doctor asked me questions. Did I know who I was? Did I know what day it was? Could I hear him? I wanted to answer but could not figure out how to make my mouth work. Then the nurse ran her scissors up the center of my T-shirt, filleting it open.

"Stop."

It was the first thing that I had said and it must have sounded terrible, perhaps not even coherent. But that shirt meant more to me than any possession I owned. Dark green, faded pale from constant wear, it was my Outward Bound shirt. The one I had earned in Minnesota. Although I could not have explained it at the time, that shirt represented a future that I had dreamed, a future in which I belonged; a life in which I was valued, good, and loveable. Now that life was being stripped from me. I would never belong, never be good or loveable again. Although I would one day work for Outward Bound, and own several of those T-shirts with the compass rose on the breast, none would ever replace the one cut from me that morning.

Attempting to speak had caused hot pain to shoot through the right side of my face. My eyes watered and my vision clouded. I considered whether or not I should try again, when the curtain beside me pulled back. Rita was gone.

Above the emergency room door hung a large clock. *Remember the time.*

I knew the moment was important but I did not know why; the trauma to my face and head had slowed and jumbled my thinking. But as my brain made the necessary connections, a rush of strength, born in the need to know, rose in me. I interrupted the doctor who was speaking to a nurse.

"Did Rita die?"

A strange look moved like a cloud across his face. Maybe he was trying to understand a question garbled by my injuries or perhaps it was the shadow of his discomfort that I saw, his reluctance to answer. I can't be sure, but my world stood still as I waited for him to speak.

"Yes," he finally said, "your friend died."

Although I wanted the doctor's answer, and in some way already knew what it would be, I was unprepared to hear his words. They entered me the way a stone falls down an empty well, bounding loudly at first, then softer and softer until I could no longer hear him at all, only watch the movement of his lips.

"Your friend," he repeated slowly, "is dead."

When I close my eyes, I can still see the face of that clock and the face of that doctor but I have never, not once in all these years, been able to see the time or hear the words he spoke.

The Funeral

My parents and I had driven across town in silence: no conversation, no radio, just the fluttering hum of the air conditioner cooling the car. We were silent because none of us knew what to say. My father was afraid to speak lest he upset me. My mother was afraid to speak lest she upset him. And for me to say anything to anyone, with my swollen face and my jaw wired shut, simply took too much effort. Each of us decided that silence was the safest way to navigate this new terrain in our lives.

Shielding my eyes, I stepped from the car into the church parking lot. Strong morning light glanced with photographic flash off the chrome bumpers. The smell of asphalt softening beneath our feet wafted up and mixed with my father's Old Spice aftershave and my mother's Chanel perfume. I would have welcomed a breath of fresh air, but the day was hot and the air still. My father slammed the car doors behind us and I winced. The sound flew back and forth inside my skull like a bird trapped in a small room. Everything seemed harsh: sounds, smells, the brightness of light, even touch grated, more than it soothed. It was as if I wore no skin. Maybe the doctor had been right, and coming to Rita's funeral was a mistake. I must have swayed a little, because my mother reached for me, but instead of taking her hand, I steadied myself against the car. I was determined to prove that I could do this.

Earlier that morning I had insisted that my mother intercede on my behalf.

"Tell him it's not for very long," I had said to her, hissing the words angrily through the small spaces of my teeth. I hated the sound of my voice imprisoned in a mouth that would remain shut for the rest of the summer.

"Honey, I don't know if you should go."

"I have to. Tell him I'm going."

"Honey."

"Just tell him."

My mother's face darkened and she sighed heavily as she met the force of my insistence. Leaving me with my chicken broth and my orange juice, she went to find the doctor making his rounds.

The years that she had been a fashion model were still evident in her walk that morning: the straight back, small steps, and careful grace. Tailored clothes flattered her still slender figure. Yet as I watched her go, I could also see a sag in her shoulders, a sag for which I felt responsible. I had made an enormous mistake and everywhere I looked, I saw the mark of it on the people I loved. I could see it in their eyes when they glanced away from me. I could hear it in their voices that were too bright over the phone. It was present in the silences between us and in the unrelated comments that swept us away from topics that might be uncomfortable.

As my mother disappeared down the hospital hallway, my anger abated and in its place my love for her welled. I swallowed hard. Crying felt dangerous; I might choke on my tears. It was safer and easier to feel edgy and short. And with no one was I shorter than with my mother. Our most innocent and well-meaning interactions could suddenly unleash a storm in me. I was full of irrational feelings, feelings that desperately needed expression, but at the time nothing made any sense. I was too young to understand my need; I only knew my mother's love was unfailing.

In the church parking lot, I held on to the top of our car until I felt steady. It had been 4 days since I had felt summer's heat, smelled anything other than antiseptic and starch, or stood on my own unaided for more than a few minutes. It's no wonder I felt overwhelmed. On the one hand, things seemed familiar; this could be any summer morning, any Mass, but it was not. As the three of us walked slowly towards the steps and the open doors of St. Theresa of the Little Flower Catholic Church, I went over the facts in my mind, as if I was rehearsing, in case someone asked. It's Monday morning. This is the funeral of Rita Ernstes. She died in an automobile accident last Thursday. I was the driver.

With my father on my left and my mother on my right, we walked through the open doors and into the dimly lit vestibule. The organ struck deep chords in a minor key, the opening of a requiem, the Mass for the dead.

Out of habit I dipped my fingers into the holy water font. The marble felt cold and smooth and when I touched the water to my forehead, I closed my eyes to feel its liquid coolness spread across my brow.

"Here," my father whispered, nodding to some empty seats in the last pew. He preferred the back of the church, especially if he was entering late or wanting to slip out quickly.

"No," I said. "I want to sit closer."

He took my arm gently but firmly, and steered me towards the pew.

I stopped and pulled away from his grasp. Narrowing my eyes, I stopped him with a voice he had not heard before, one that was hushed, bitter, and defiant. "She was my friend. We're sitting down in front."

My mother, afraid of an escalating scene, intervened. "Billy, please," she whispered.

A look passed between them, a moment where something was decided. In our life together as a family, I had seen that look many times; it was a pleading look, one that she used to postpone a skirmish until later.

"Fine, you run the show then," he muttered beneath his breath, taking a step back from the two of us, hurt and angry. My mother then moved to his side and slipped her arm through his. It was her way of reassuring him that he was necessary, and of evening the balance between them. Then she reached out to me. This time I accepted her hand and the three of us walked together to the front of the church.

On either side of the aisle, men sat sweating in their dark jackets while women fanned themselves with folded church bulletins and children squirmed. Everyone seemed restless in the heat. It's easy to think that people stared at us, nodded in our direction, or raised their eyebrows with one another knowingly. I knew that I had been "the driver," the one who caused the accident, and I was sure that everyone else knew it too. Those few dozen steps, from the back of the church to the front, seemed like miles. The air was thick with incense, somber music, and grief—and all of it pressed down on me.

After what seemed like forever, we reached the front pew where Rita's entire family was kneeling. A few of their blonde heads turned. Mr. Ernstes clenched his jaw and had to turn away. Claire's eyes were red from crying while Becky's face was a blank mask. Who had I become to them? Did they hate me? I stood frozen in the aisle while my mother and father genuflected and started to enter the pew behind Rita's family. Abruptly, Mrs. Ernstes lifted herself heavily from her knees and stood. She smoothed her dress and turned to me. With one hand she gestured for me to sit with them, with the other she gripped the pew.

What I most wanted was to simply follow my parents, to sit with them, but I could not make my feet move. I looked at Rita's mother standing, motioning to me, and remembered her on their front porch a few mornings before, clutching her housecoat, insisting Rita take the blanket she offered. I had to sit with Rita's family. A wave of nausea rolled through me as I slid first, in front of Rita's dad, next, in front of her little brother, her oldest sister, and then her mother. It was a relief to finally sit down as I settled next to Mrs. Ernstes, between her and Becky. Meanwhile, my own mother and father knelt alone in the pew behind. The entrance hymn soared and all the church stood as the priest entered.

Over the years I have come to see how utterly responsible I felt for Rita's death and as a result how determined I was to accept whatever consequences were necessary. And since no consequences were imposed upon me, I created my own. Like a penance, I assigned myself the following rules: be kind, be grateful, be strong; do not feel, expect, or need anything; do not make mistakes and most of all, never cause such harm again. I began my penance that morning, by sitting uneasily with the Ernstes family rather than in the comfort of my own. Over the next 20 years, this way of living would still add up to only the smallest of payments against the enormous debt I believed I owed.

By now the priest had circled the sanctuary swinging an incense burner, and had descended the steps to stand in front of Rita's casket. I hadn't noticed the long metal box, draped in white linen, a bouquet of lilies lying on its top, until the priest stood before it. I stared at it for a long time. Somewhere in the far back of my mind, a voice spoke: "Rita is in that box and she's never coming out." As time passed another line would be added. "And, it's your fault."

The chain on the incense burner clanked as the priest swung it out and then back, out and then back. The smoke thickened and rose, drifting upward into a shaft of crimson-colored light. I watched as the red stained glass window turned like a kaleidoscope, its shapes and colors revolving and shifting. Years later, a therapist explained that I had done exactly what people do in order to get through such an emotionally overpowering experience.

"They focus on some small detail," she said. "They don't think about anything and they don't feel."

So I got lost in the beauty of a stained glass window while the Mass proceeded. From years of habit, I managed to recite all the prayers, to kneel and stand in all the right places, to listen without hearing.

"Eternal rest grant unto her, Oh Lord." The priest spoke solemnly with his arms outstretched and hands slightly lifted over Rita's casket.

41

"And may perpetual light shine upon her," everyone replied. I heard myself say the words and looked around, seeing things as if for the first time.

"May the soul of Rita Ernstes rest in peace."

"Amen," we answered.

The words sealed the ritual, as if to say: "It is over." But nothing felt over inside of me. Rita's family followed the casket out of the church and on to the cemetery. My parents drove me back to the hospital. "Amen," I whispered. "Amen." The words echoed off the hollowness of my heart until they began colliding with one another.

When I finally reached my hospital room, I was soaked with sweat. My mother went to get a cup of coffee while a nurse helped me back into bed.

"Are you in pain?" she asked, taking my pulse and looking at me with concern.

I nodded.

She placed a cool cloth on my forehead, raised a syringe, and pushed the plunger in to insure no air remained. The little spray of liquid shooting from the needle fractured in the midday light. "Amen," I whispered once more.

"What?" the nurse asked leaning over me, but I was drifting away.

Memory and Dream

I awoke to my mother's hand on my shoulder. "Honey, I'm going home now," she said softly. "I'll be back in the morning." She kissed my forehead.

"Mom, do you still love me?"

"Oh, honey. Of course I love you." Tears filled her eyes. Then she took my hand, held it a moment, and gave it a squeeze. "You rest. I will be back in the morning."

It wasn't so much her words, but my hand in hers that comforted me. I lay in the dark for a while after she left, listening to the night sounds of the hospital. I could still feel my hand in hers when I remembered my first midnight Mass. The year was 1961 and I was 6 years old. What began as memory, a recalling of something in the past, became a dream, vivid and real.

…I am driving with my mom and dad to my grandparents' house for Christmas Eve dinner. A light snow is falling and we are riding in our new car whose make and model I have been repeating to myself over and over, in the back seat. There is something about the way it sounds that I recognize: *Buick Electra, two-twenty-five. Buick Electra, two-twenty-five.* Finally, as we turn up my grandparents' street, it registers.

"It's like our telephone number!" I blurt.

My father turns the music down as my mother turns her head; the movement stirs the air so that her perfume drifts my way.

"What, honey?"

Now the backseat smells like her. "It sounds like our phone number: At-Water, three-six, two-two-oh," I explain, pleased by having solved my little puzzle.

I am so proud that I don't see my mother's confusion or my father's shoulders shrug as their eyes meet. I am already off, thinking new thoughts, having figured out the rhythm mystery of our new car's name. Now I am thinking about snow forts, sledding, what Santa is bringing.

Bing Crosby sings on the radio and my father wonders aloud if the snow will stick as we turn up the long straight drive to "forty-four hundred." That's how my parents refer to the large white house where my grandparents live.

"It's so pretty," my mother says, referring to the way the snow sticks in some places and sifts away in others, "like flour on a bread-board."

I watch the white flakes swirl and dance in the headlights as we park the car. I don't wait for my father to open my door. Instead I pull on the handle, push the door open with my foot, and climb out. I am clutching my grandfather's package tightly in my hand.

While my father escorts my mother, who steps carefully in her red stiletto heels, I skate towards the back door on the slick soles of my patent leather shoes. My gray wool coat, unbuttoned, billows behind me like a cape and I hold my grandfather's gift, a tie wrapped in gold foil paper, out beside me for balance. *I am a lot to handle,* at least that is what I overhear my mother say to her sister, whenever they talk. When she says this, she is speaking of the part of me that is always on the go: I run everywhere, roar down the street on my bike, move fast whenever I can.

Standing beside my grandparents' back porch steps is a statue of St. Francis. Snow has accumulated on his shoulders, the top of his head, as well as on the backs of the little birds that he cups in his hands Taking the steps two at a time, I mumble a prayer for the poor people like I have been taught in school. I add one for the birds as well, though no one has told me to do so. Then, I stop and wait.

I wait because that is what grown-ups do; they wait for one another. And tonight, I am feeling very grown up. Later, after Christmas Eve dinner with my father's family, I will go to midnight Mass. Even though I am only in first grade, I have recently realized that the whole Christmas story takes place at night: with shepherds keeping watch over their flocks, wise men following a star, and the holy family camping out in a stable. Armed with the firm conviction that Jesus was born at night, I had lobbied my mom and dad throughout Advent.

"We have to go at midnight!" I would plead, following my mom as she carried laundry up the stairs from the basement.

"It's when Jesus was really born, Dad," I would insist for the hundredth time as he raked leaves from beneath the oak tree in our yard. "If we wait 'til Christmas morning, it's too late."

Worn down by my persistence and zealous belief that this change in our family tradition was of great spiritual importance, the two of them relented. There are few Catholics more devout than those in first grade.

"Watch it, Cay," my father says, his voice edged with anxiety that sounds like impatience. He has my mother by the arm so she won't slip in her high heels. My parents are beautiful to me. My mother is 26, tall and slender in a red knit dress, black wool coat, and a red pillbox hat, emulating the style of the current First Lady. I think my mother is prettier than "Jackie"—and my father, much more handsome than "Jack." That is how Mom and Dad refer to the President and his wife, by their first names. They are Catholics too.

My father is 30, tall in a black topcoat; his black Irish blood shows in his olive complexion, his dark eyebrows, and almost black hair. I am a miniature version of my parents, inheriting my mother's easygoing temperament and my father's features and looks. Tall for my age, I am a complete tomboy ready for action even though tonight I am dressed in a green velvet skirt and white blouse.

"Come on, you guys," I urge, excited and anxious to go inside. The two of them continue to walk slowly and carefully across the drive, leaning on one another the way they do in life.

Billy Johnson, my father, is the oldest son of Karl and Rosemary Johnson. The Johnsons are a large Irish Catholic family of some importance in our town. My father is a good son; as a young man, he helped his folks raise his sister and four of six brothers before leaving home for college at Notre Dame, the Marine Corps, and Korean War. When he returned from the war, he married my mother. I was born 9 months later and was 2 months old when my grandmother delivered her eighth and last child, my uncle Steve. I never thought it unusual that many of my uncles were close to me in age—or in Stevie's case, younger.

As my parents pass St. Francis, Uncle Stevie opens the back door. He could be my brother, we look so much alike, except that I am taller, faster, and stronger.

"Our packages are real big," Stevie says in a loud whisper that means what he has to say is important. "I can show you." He curls his index finger, beckoning me to follow him inside.

Since Stevie and I are more like brother and sister than uncle and niece, we receive identical presents at Christmas so we won't fight or feel jealous of one another. He and I do not know that this is intentional. Instead we think it's funny and coincidental that we get the same things each year.

My father nods his permission for me to go on ahead.

"Make sure to say hello to Karlyboy and Rosie," he calls out as the back door slams behind Stevie and me. Everyone calls my grandparents by their nicknames, including me.

After a quick examination, a couple of hugs, and gin-flavored kisses, Stevie and I are on our hands and knees crawling beneath the bottom branches of an enormous Christmas tree. It fills my grandparents' living room with the smell of pine and chemical flocking. Stevie starts to read tags on the presents. Neither of us has been reading for long and he is delighted to show off.

"To Paul, from Mike," he reads slowly. "To Greg, from Mom. To…" he pauses and looks at me, grinning. A red ornament hangs in front of his head, so all I can see is a big red ball with a mouth opening and closing below it. The mouth says conspiratorially, "This one's for you." I giggle and clap my hands. *What is it?* I will have to wait until after dinner to find out.

The evening is full: there are snacks everywhere—ribbon candies and nuts in little crystal dishes, plates of crackers each spread with cheese and topped with a bite-size cube of smoked ham. The grown-ups will have cocktails. My older uncles will play poker. My younger uncles will make a game of slipping by the bar when no one is looking, and pouring rum into their Coca-Colas. Stevie and I watch all this from under the Christmas tree. When the betting from the family room grows increasingly loud and more aggressive, I think my grandfather will intervene, but he and my father are talking business over martinis and appear not to notice. Meanwhile, my grandmother and mother sit on the living room couch, talking quietly, where they can keep an eye on Stevie and me.

Our traditional Christmas Eve dinner consists of turkey sandwiches, cranberries, and mashed potatoes. Finally, when we push back from the table, my grandmother announces that now we will open presents. I feel like I will explode when I slide off my chair and go running into the living room. The wait has been interminable. Soon Stevie and I are ripping into brightly wrapped boxes containing Etch-a-Sketches, coloring books, and two large 50-piece soldier sets from FAO Schwarz. Santa has brought Stevie the Union Army and me, the forces of the Confederacy. Each set comes with matching infantry cap. Stevie and I spend the rest of the evening lying on our stomachs in the middle of the living room, dressed in our best Christmas outfits, wearing our Civil War caps and playing with our soldiers. Lost in our battles, we are oblivious to the rest of the family.

Eventually, Stevie has to go to bed. My mother insists that I lie down on the couch.

"What about Mass?" I say, my lower lip starting to quiver.

"We're still going to Mass, that's why I want you to rest, so you'll be ready."

My mother kisses me on the forehead, slips my shoes off, and covers me with a light blanket. I watch the Christmas tree lights for a long time.

When I open my eyes again, I am in the back seat of our new car. Christmas carols play softly on the radio while Mom and Dad talk in low voices. I watch the red ends of their cigarettes glowing like sparklers in the dark. Outside, the snow has stopped and the sky is black and clear. From under the blanket of my backseat nest, I look at the stars, tiny white fires in a cold winter sky. Then a flashing red light moves across my view.

"Rudolph!" I yell, sitting up and pressing my face to the window.

"Honey, look." My mother points out the windshield for my father to see. "It *is* Rudolph." All the way to the church, Mom talks about how lucky we are to have spotted Santa flying over our town. "You know," my mother says, holding my hand as we walk up the church steps, "the shepherds looked up, just like you did tonight, and that's how they saw the star that they followed to baby Jesus' birth. Think how lucky they must have felt."

I try to think about how lucky the shepherds felt, but all I can feel is my own excitement, I am tingling all over. I also feel serious. Going to Mass is always serious.

Inside, the church is dimly lit. I am surprised by how many people are here, many more than on Sunday mornings. The air is thick with incense and the hushed murmurs of neighbors greeting one another. I keep thinking about what my mother has said, and thinking about Rudolph. Some part of me knows that the blinking red light was really a plane passing overhead, and yet some other part of me believes that I have also seen the most famous reindeer of all.

When the carols begin, my mother leans down and whispers in my ear, "Let's go and visit baby Jesus." She takes my hand and we walk down the side aisle to the nativity scene. As we near the manger, the star above it catches my eye. It is nothing more than a piece of cardboard cut with five points and painted gold. There is a hole in the center of it through which a single white Christmas tree light shines. When I look at the manger, I see that Baby Jesus is a toy doll. It's not real, none of it. I feel my face getting hot. I tug on Mom's arm and look up at her. She is crying.

Even though there are tears on Mom's face, she does not look sad; instead she looks happy. The candlelit church is crowded and there is something I can feel beginning, maybe something special *is* happening. Maybe that something is happening inside me. I feel warm and full like a bathtub about to run over.

"Mom!" I whisper, "Is Baby Jesus really here?" I am thinking about the doll in the manger.

"Yes, honey, he is."

"Where?"

"He's all around us, can you feel him?"

I look up then down at the center of my chest. "Mom, I think he might be in here." With my free hand I point at my heart. Mom smiles and squeezes my hand.

"Jesus loves you very much, honey, because you are such a good girl." She looks like there's more to say but instead gives my hand a little tug. "C'mon, Mass is starting."

We walk to our seats, the choir begins to sing the opening hymn: *Oh Come, Oh Come, Emmanuel.* I hold Mom's hand; her skin seems extra soft. It does not matter that the nativity star is fake. It does not matter that the blinking red light in the sky might have been an airplane, passing overhead. What matters is this feeling, this hand in mine, this moment. I know somehow that this moment is the best Christmas gift I have ever gotten—way better than a soldier set.

The next morning I was discharged from the hospital. And, it's clear to me now that it wasn't so much whether my mother still loved me; what I really wanted to know was whether or not God did.

RECOVERY

Two days after Rita's funeral, I came home from the hospital. At first it was easy to follow the doctor's order for bed rest; I had little energy and it was painful to concentrate. When I tried to read, words distorted and disappeared in halos of white light. Television was worse. After a few minutes, the flickering images left my eyes burning and head splitting. Gratefully, during those first few days at home, I mostly slept. I did not think about Rita or Becky, the accident, the funeral, or camp.

Maybe I was blessed, or maybe a wiser part of me knew that to think about anything, anything at all, would have thrown me into a bleak terrain: an emotional landscape where nothing lived, nothing mattered, and no hope grew. So, instead of thinking, I daydreamed. I recalled in vivid detail all the wild places that I had traveled: the Florida Everglades where dark roots reach like great talons into bracken water, and flocks of stilt-legged birds fly before petal-pink dawns. I pictured the mirror-still lakes of Minnesota where summer raindrops fall like quicksilver pebbles, hitting the water with a plunk and the bottom of an aluminum canoe with a ping. Over time I imagined new vistas, places I had never been but hoped to one day go: Alaska, Utah, Yellowstone, the Grand Canyon. Just by saying the names of these places, I could envision their snowy mountains, green rivers, great forests, and red rock canyons. This was how I passed my days, the hours between wakefulness and sleep, by mapping a pilgrimage that would eventually take me along the beaches and blue highways, the craggy mountains and empty deserts of this country. By learning to travel in wild places, maybe I could learn to navigate the stark territory within.

After a week in the dim light of my basement bedroom, I started craving fresh air and sunlight. Finally, one afternoon I decided to get up. At the time it seemed like an enormous decision and an incredible challenge, to get out of bed, go upstairs, and walk outside. That first spark of determination was both fragile and persistent.

Swinging my legs down beside the bed, I sat up, then stood. Immediately, I had to sit back down. A framed map of the Boundary Waters Canoe Area on my bedroom wall appeared like a large abstract painting done in yellow and blue, and pulled up to my desk were two chairs instead of one. After a couple of seconds though, my vision cleared. The blue lakes of northern Minnesota returned and a single chair appeared before me. I grabbed ahold of it and tried standing again. This time the room stayed solid.

Dragging a light cotton throw, I made my way upstairs into the bright and expansive world of my parents. The carpet in the living room was plush and bright yellow, the sofa, plump and eggshell white. Modern paintings in primary colors hung on moon-white walls and at the end of the room, large windows stood from floor to ceiling, looking over small green fields and a narrow lane into a woodland beyond. I blinked and squinted as if I was seeing it anew. It was a feeling I would come to know well whenever I felt vulnerable, one of being a stranger in the most familiar of places.

Crossing the living room into the dining area, I moved towards our back deck. I could hear my mother in the kitchen fixing dinner and humming a Burt Bacharach tune. I should have said something to her but I wanted to slip by unnoticed, to avoid her attention. I needed to feel capable. But, just as I reached for the handle of the sliding deck door, the corner of the throw caught on the leg of a sideboard that served as a liquor cabinet. The small resistance jerked me back and nearly pulled me over. I cursed, gathered my strength, and tugged on the blanket. The sideboard shook, bottles clinked, and a highball glass went crashing to the floor. My mother let out a startled sound, but I was already out the door and onto the deck.

I felt triumphant even if just for a moment. Then I collapsed into a lounge chair. Instantly, my mother was beside me, tucking in the blanket, saying I should have called her, shouldn't have gotten up without her help, what was I thinking? But I was not listening. The afternoon light was filtering through the woods, throwing long shadows down the tree-lined lane. I could smell charcoal heating on a neighbor's grill, hear the slam of a car door and the call of a blackbird. In that moment I knew the difference between a daydream and a real dream. Being outside was real and it was exactly the medicine I needed.

For most of the next week, I rested on our back deck. Built one story above ground level, the 15x10-foot space was ideal for summer use. Open and airy, it was decorated with iron patio furniture: a couple of lounge chairs for sunbathing, a small café table with straight-back chairs for chess games and cocktails. Large pots in each corner held hearty bougainvillea with pomegranate-colored blossoms. Nature added an ancient broadleaf maple just beyond the deck's railing. With a thick gray trunk and wide dense canopy, the tree would ignite with emerald fire in the morning. By midday it provided much needed shade and in the cool of the evening, it filled with songbirds twittering, frittering, whistling themselves towards sleep. From either lounge chair I could watch the changing light and the comings and goings in the green world of that maple. When I wanted to travel, I could look across rolling grass down the lane. Like a road in a painting, this one, too, drew the eye away. It stretched and narrowed until it was no more than a thin line disappearing out of sight.

I regained both my strength and my balance. Now, in the mornings, I would get up, bathe, dress, and get my own juice from the refrigerator. But who was the "I" who did these things? Some part of me seemed to be observing the rest. I felt disconnected from my actions and what I saw and heard around me. Even though I spent hours staring at the trees, the light, the sky, or listening to the wind, the birds, the neighbor's chimes, I was not aware of being touched or soothed by them. It was as if I watched and listened without seeing or hearing. I spent a string of days like that, lying out on the deck letting the minutes pass like clouds, the hours like the movement of the sun. Before I knew it another day would be over. In this way I also avoided my parents and in some ways they avoided me. It was easier not to interact, since I could barely speak and none of us knew what to say.

Then one morning, something changed. I was staring at a straw that rested undisturbed against the rim of my juice glass. Even though it was only a few feet from me, it appeared to be a long way off, watery and odd-looking. Since my vision had been fine for some time, I thought it odd that the straw appeared this way.

Plastic drinking straws had become a routine artifact in my life with a broken jaw. They were ever-present at my bedside and in front of me at every meal. Eventually, I would stash them in books and dresser drawers; leave them on windowsills and countertops; carry a box in the glove compartment and a bundle in my guitar case. But in the early days after the accident, I knew them best as my bedside companions. And because they were such a constant, I never considered them—until now.

Blinking several times, the straw came into better focus. *That was weird,* I thought, realizing how long it had been since I had really noticed something. All the everyday voices of internal commentary, self-conversations, and regular reflections had been absent until now. All at once, my mind raced like a river freed from a jam. Within seconds, my head was filled with a torrent of thoughts, ideas, and realizations.

My friends were all at camp. I was here, recovering. *Recovering from what?* My mouth would be wired shut for the rest of the summer, but otherwise I knew I was well. *What am I still doing here? I should be at camp.*

The urge to be with my friends was great, but even greater was the urge to be on the land where I had spent every summer since I was 7 years old. Some part of me that had been "away" returned, and now she was gathering the rest of me up and taking me with her. I did not think about what had happened or what had been lost, only about what I had to do.

It must be close to eleven, I thought, as I threw off the blanket that covered me. Out of habit, I looked at my wrist. It was bare. I had not worn a watch since mine had been removed in the emergency room. Until that moment, I hadn't noticed. Now I wanted to know what time it was, what day, where I was going, and how would I get there?

My mother was talking on the phone as I came inside. At the time, she managed the apartments where we lived and was always negotiating with painters, electricians, and plumbers. Without hesitation, I walked through the living room, down the stairs past her office, and into my room.

Searching unsuccessfully for my watch on both my dresser and desk, I tried the bathroom, thinking it might be on the sink, or back of the toilet. It was not in those places either. I turned to go, then stopped. In the mirror, a tall young woman with small breasts and broad shoulders that rounded slightly forward stood before me. "Stand up straight!" I could hear my mother's voice in my head and without thinking, obediently stood taller. My long brown hair was pulled back and clipped up. I leaned closer to the mirror.

In my early adolescence I had experimented with the usual habits of feminine beauty: the shaving, plucking, painting, and pinching. A lot of it hurt, and the outcomes seemed negligible. As a result, at 18, I did none of it. But as I inspected the bright pink skin stretching tightly over the places where nasty lacerations had healed, I understood why someone would want to hide the marks that blemished them. A dark smudge, the last of the bruising, ran the length of my jaw and left a shadow beneath my right eye. The lower right side of my face bulged, still swollen from surgery. I looked as if I had a wad of chewing tobacco sitting in my lower lip. Each day I looked better, more normal. Yet it was obvious that something had happened to my face, and I wished

55

that I could hide the fact. Not because the marks detracted from my looks, but because they made me feel so vulnerable.

I tried a smile. My lips parted and the braces that wired my top and bottom teeth together glinted in the harsh light of the bathroom. *That's hideous.* I practiced a smaller smile, one that left my lips closed over my teeth. When I felt satisfied with the result, I tried speaking. "Hey. How's it goin'?" The words buzzed against my teeth. I tried the same greeting a little louder, hoping for less buzz.

"Honey? Is that you?" my mother called from her upstairs office.

Couldn't I have a little privacy! A sense of angry urgency now fueled my determination to leave. I interpreted my mother's simple question as prying, evidence that I would be better off at camp. I couldn't stay at home any longer. At camp my days would be busy, my life have a purpose. My mother's attentions threatened my 18-year-old need for independence as well as my need to run away from what had happened. Later in life I would long for the tenderness my mother offered that day: a tenderness that I could not accept.

My mother's office was nothing more than a large utility closet converted for her use, with a desk, copy machine, file cabinet, and bookshelves. I stood in the doorway. My mother sat at her desk, talking on the phone. Neat piles of paper surrounded her. A cigarette smoldered in a glass ashtray. For a minute or two I watched its smoke curl upward. But I was not content to wait; I went and sat down in the chair beside her desk. Immediately she looked at me, smiled, and rolled her eyes.

"Uh-huh, uh-huh," she said.

Clearly she was stuck in a one-way conversation, probably with a tenant complaining about something or other. My mother, who was always extremely polite, listened without interrupting. The thought that this conversation could go on forever made me anxious. Waiting was not possible. I bent forward, pursed my lips, and furrowed my brow, letting her know that I wanted to talk to her—now!

She got the message. "Yes, well I really do have to go, but I'll take care of it, before the end of the week." Hanging up the phone, she turned to me, looking a little irritated or maybe just concerned. "What's wrong?"

"I want to go back to camp." The words hurried from me. Two weeks of the 8-week camp season were nearly finished. I felt sure I had already missed everything. What if my friends forgot me, what if there was no place for me?

"We can call Father Schneider on Monday."

"No. Call him now. Please? I want to work next week." My mother's eyes darkened. She frowned and shook her head from side to side. "Please?" I persisted. "I can't stay here any longer; I'm going crazy."

My mother had always had trouble saying "No" to me. She would tell people that it was because I rarely asked for anything unreasonable, that I carried a sensibility that seemed wise beyond my years.

She sighed, turned back to her desk, opened her address book, and dialed the camp number.

A great wave of relief washed over me. I let out a breath that I had been holding, maybe for days. "I love you, Mom."

She nodded, dabbing at her eyes while she listened into the receiver for someone on the other end to answer.

"Father Schneider, please."

I imagined Janie the camp director picking up the phone. She would be in the camp's office, located in the Priests' House. I could see the worn sofa, mismatched easy chairs, the knotty pine walls, and the picture of the Sacred Heart of Jesus hanging over the desk. We had had some good parties in that living room when Father was away, the sacred heart, the sacred beer, the sacred pranks we conceived of and later played on those not present.

"No, I don't mind." My mother turned in her chair. "He's cutting the grass."

It was nearly noon. Father would probably be finishing up the front field. I could see him stopped, sitting on the tractor surveying his work. The baseball cap he wore to protect his balding head and fair skin would be rimmed with sweat. He was always red faced, sunburned in spite of his attempts to shade himself. He would fill his pipe from the soft black leather pouch he kept in the back pocket of his jeans, and then puffing plumes of sweet smoke would hear Janie's yell, wave to her, and start the tractor again, turning its big round wheel towards the main part of camp. Like a movie I had watched a hundred times, I could see the scene unfold, accompanied by a soundtrack of little girls shrieking and laughing.

"Father? This is Cay Johnson calling. I'm fine. Thank you. She's fine too. That is why I'm calling. Cathy would like to come back to work."

Seconds seemed to pass like minutes. My heart beat faster. What was he saying to her? My mother had a grave look on her face as she listened. I knew something wasn't right. Finally, after what seemed like forever, she spoke.

"Yes, of course, I understand. I will talk to her and call you back."

My mother replaced the phone's receiver in its cradle slowly and softly. Then she faced me.

"Father's not sure you are ready to come back."

I sat back in my chair, as if I had been shoved. This was not what I expected.

"What do you mean, not ready? What does he know about how I am?"

"Honey, he wants you to understand that camp is a job, not just a place where you go to be with your friends."

"I know that!"

"He's worried you're not physically ready. It's only been two weeks."

"It's been more than two."

My mother's office felt airless. I grabbed her arm. It hadn't occurred to me that I wouldn't be able to go back to camp. I began to cry.

"Mom, please. Please let me go."

She did not answer, but looked at me in a way that I will never forget: her face tight, her eyes dark. She knew that returning to camp would make me happy. Yet she harbored a vague reservation. Years later she confessed that she worried about me being in the company of Rita's sisters and friends, that they would serve as a constant reminder of the accident and what if that was too much? Whatever her worry, she left it in her heart.

"OK. I'll call Father back."

Feelings flooded me: gratitude, relief, love. On some level my mother knew I needed help; that was the reservation she was unable to name. And, how could she name what she had not known or could imagine for herself. I came from a family uncomfortable with grief; who had to suffer mine in a time when counseling was unheard of and getting on with life was the common expectation.

Sitting very still, I listened as her conversation with Father began. He seemed to be yielding as she addressed his concerns. Feeling more relaxed, I sat back and began to picture scenes from camp. I imagined all the kids running to line up for afternoon canteen, Becky riding up on horseback from the barn, a small water fight in the creek that was just waiting to spill over the banks and involve the entire camp.

"Honey?" My mother was holding the phone out to me. "Father wants to talk to you."

I felt like I had been caught in school not paying attention as I took the phone from her hand. "Hello?" I said cautiously.

Father Schneider was a nice man, a kind man, a good priest who worked hard. When he said Mass, he made his sermons meaningful and relevant to the times and to his congregation of girls and young women. He tried to be warm and affectionate, but there was often an underlying awkwardness in his interactions. Perhaps it was disturbing being surrounded by so much female adolescent beauty. And, like many men, Father reacted with anger when he felt afraid. In those days, I just thought he had a short temper.

"Cathy," he launched, speaking sternly. "I want to be very clear with you. If you come down here, you come down to work. There won't be anyone to take care of you."

Did he think I needed a nurse? "I don't need anyone to take care of me, Father. You don't have to worry."

"There's not going to be time to talk about things."

He avoided saying *the accident, your feelings, Rita's death*, but we both knew to which "things" he was referring. My voice lowered, "I don't need to talk about things."

"Promise?"

In my memory his question hangs like a door. At the time it was the only one I could see to walk through.

"I promise," I said.

For the rest of that summer and the next 18 years of my life, I spoke little, if ever, about the accident, nor did I cry for what had been lost. In my work and relationships I tried to be as independent, and make as little trouble, as possible. I made a promise to a priest and let that promise shape my life.

Return to Camp

I have always packed more than I need, and after the accident the habit became even more pronounced. Now, more than ever, I wanted to feel prepared and be surrounded by comforting things.

Stuffing my beloved Notre Dame sweatshirt with tattered cuffs and mended tears into a by-then full duffel, I strained to cinch the top closed. Finally satisfied that the heavy canvas bag would remain closed, I dragged it up the stairs and stood it by the front door. My guitar case was there, along with a small tower of cardboard boxes, each one filled with cans of cream of potato soup, my dietary staple.

In the 3 weeks following surgery on my jaw, I lost 15 pounds. When the doctor noted the weight I had dropped, he tried to bolster my culinary courage.

"People blend up all sorts of things," he said, "even hamburgers and pizza."

But the only thing that tasted any good to me, sucked through a straw, was cream of potato soup. I ate it for breakfast, lunch, and dinner without variation. Its thick creamy warmth was comforting and its salty flavor satisfying.

Along with my soup, clothes, and guitar was a metal milk crate filled with a loose assortment of items intended to add ambience to our counselors' cabin. There was a tape player and box of cassette tapes: Joni Mitchell, Leonard Cohen, and Bob Dylan. There was a black light, some incense, and a poster entitled "Desiderata" which displayed an inscription: *Go placidly amid the noise and haste... Remember what peace may be found in silence... You have a right to be here.* Could I believe that I had a right to be here, to be alive in the wake of what had happened? There are signs along the way that guide us through our suffering, whether we notice them or not. Those lines were a subtle reminder that my life had value.

I added one last thing to the crate, a folded Navajo blanket that my uncle Greg gave me earlier that spring when he visited. The blanket smelled like sagebrush and carried the colors of the northern Arizona desert: stripes of red rock and sky, sunset and sand.

Greg was one of my father's younger brothers; 16 years and a whole world stood between the two of them, but they kept in touch as if they shared a special bond. With long black hair, bare feet, a drug habit, and burned draft card, Greg was the son no longer welcome in my grandfather's house. Wealthy, Catholic, and conservative, my grandparents were frightened by the social upheaval of the '60s. In my father, their eldest son, they were reassured seeing a younger version of themselves. In Greg, they saw their age and their insecurity and everything they could not control. Greg kept in touch with the family by stopping at our house whenever he came into town.

On his spring visit, after a couple of beers, he asked my father for money. My father turned him down, their bond strained by Greg's lifestyle and increasing drug use. His request denied, Greg drained the last of his beer and a few minutes later said that he had to go. I followed my father and his brother outside. Just a month away from my eighteenth birthday, I was eager to be away from home, as free as I perceived Greg to be. I was curious about drugs and listened with intent interest to his stories of rock concerts and road trips. At some level, by watching my father and Greg, I was learning about my father's tolerance for deviance, gauging how far I might drift from his norms, before risking his rejection.

The two brothers said their goodbyes. My father started back to the house, then stopped, changing his mind about something. He reached into his wallet, removed a $50 bill, and gave it to Greg. The look on Greg's face was one of true gratitude.

"I'll pay you back, Billy, soon as I get ahead."

"Forget it. Just get your shit together; you're worrying Mom and Dad."

With that said, my father walked away, leaving me standing alone with my uncle.

"Your dad can sure be uptight, but he's also pretty cool." Greg's eyes caught mine. He smiled, opened the back of his beat-up van, and impulsively pulled out a woven blanket. "Here, this is for you." He gave me a hug and then said in a softer voice: "You take care; and tell Billy I love him."

Holding the blanket, I watched Greg drive away. He was heading for Texas, maybe California. I envied him. I could not see the murkier waters running beneath the surface of Greg's carefree life. He was a lost soul. It's true he could travel anywhere, but in reality, he had nowhere to go.

Not long after that visit, Greg went to prison for trafficking drugs and I had my accident. Now we were both lost. I placed his blanket in the milk crate, the poster back on top, and went to tell my mother that I was ready to go.

"Mom," I called, buzzing like a kazoo. "Mom, I'm ready." No answer. I headed through the living room to check in the kitchen. "Mom?" I called louder, the word vibrating against my teeth. Grabbing a straw from the counter, a Coke from the refrigerator, and shutting the door with my foot, I wondered how I would ever yell loud enough at camp. How would I get the kids' attention? My usually booming voice was muffled inside my mouth. "Mom, are you up there?" *You'll figure it out*, I told myself, taking the stairs two at a time and pushing open the door to my parents' bedroom. My mother was sitting on the bed, holding the phone on her lap. She turned when I came in; I could see that she had been crying.

"Mom?"

"Your father is on the way, he wants us to wait."

"What's wrong?"

"Nothing's wrong, sweetheart; he has something he wants to give you before you leave."

My mother stood, smoothing the front of her blouse, re-tucking it into the waistband of her pale blue Bermuda shorts.

"I need a little lipstick," she said and walked into their bathroom.

As I watched my mother check her makeup, I remembered the stories she had told me about watching her own mother through holes drilled in a bedroom door. My grandmother was an invalid infected with tuberculosis from the time my mother was 8 until she died, just before my mother's thirteenth birthday. During those 4 years, my mother only knew her own through little windows, one inch round.

How my mother must have longed to crawl into her mother's lap, to have long talks or arm-in-arm walks. In that moment, watching her across the room freshening her makeup and combing her hair, I could feel the same longing. I wanted to ask her why she was crying; was she disappointed in me? I wanted her to tell me that she loved me and that everything would be OK. But we had always avoided uncomfortable topics: the ones that might dredge up hurt or ignite anger. Neither of us knew how to hold the feelings of the other without assuming responsibility for them. In that way, there might as well have been a door between us too.

During the years that her mother was sick, my mother must have felt frightened, perhaps angry or sad. Yet, whenever I asked my mother what it was like for her as a child, she would look away, give a little sigh, and say:

"Oh honey, I don't know. We just got on with things; that's what you did in those days."

Those days were no different from the ones we were living now. Getting on with things had become the primary objective. No one needed to tell me. I simply knew that was what I was supposed to do. I knew it in the way that family members do. The rules and expectations, whether spoken or not, are simply understood. The message was as clear as if delivered by God: do not feel, focus on living instead, forget about Rita's death; forget that the accident ever occurred. It took years to understand how I, like my mother before me, and who knows how many of her Irish kin, shuttered the room where pain lived, locked the door, and turned away. Although my mother had crossed the country of loss many times in her life, she had no map for grieving. How could she help me do what she had never done?

If my mother and I skirted difficult topics, my father avoided them altogether. He could not tolerate emotional pain of any kind. He was one of those men whose helplessness left him, at best anxious, at worst frustrated and irate. He needed to feel in control and always tried to do the right thing. He took care of his younger brothers, served as an altar boy and later as a Marine in Korea. When he mustered out of the Marine Corps, he went to work for his father. Tall and handsome, he used his charm and native intelligence to make his way in the world. But underneath his good looks, sharp clothes, and funny jokes, he was a man who could barely read or write, a man who lacked confidence in himself and what he could accomplish.

As a child I did not see my father's complexities, only his love. I adored him and made allowances for his rage. My father would bottle his daily frustrations and disappointments until some triggering event: a dinner served late or a chore forgotten unleashed a verbal fury that would rip through the house, like a knife through cloth. As a result, my mother and I spent an enormous amount of energy trying to keep everything perfect and calm for him. Though my father knew the facts of my life, he knew few of its heartfelt truths.

My mother and father were overwhelmed by the accident, frightened by what had happened, and completely at a loss how to help. My father only visited me once in the hospital, gave me a kiss on the forehead, and left quickly. It was the best he could do. Once at home, he focused on the future, my going off to college in the fall, a trip for the three of us to Florida at Christmas. He just wanted everything to return to normal. For me, though, life would never again be normal.

Mom came out of the bathroom just as the sound of cars pulling up in the driveway drifted up to the bedroom.

"That's probably Dad now."

I got up from their bed and started for the door.

"Honey," she said, then stopped as if she wanted to say more but did not know how.

"Cathy, Cay?" my father's voice yelled pleasantly from the front hallway.

"Go on," she sighed, nodding towards the bedroom door.

"Hey Dad." I rounded the corner into the hallway. My mother hung slightly back. Her tears had to do with this moment. I looked at her as I hugged my father, but could not understand.

"Put your stuff in the car. I've got something for you."

His tone of voice was familiar, a little mischievous and excited. What could he have for me that was so important that he would leave early on a Sunday morning to go and get? Eager to know, I hoisted my duffel bag and opened the front door. There, parked in the driveway was a brand new Jeep.

I felt as if all the air had left the world, as if I were pinned against an invisible wall. *This is crazy*, I wanted to say. *Crazy!* I wanted to scream and cry, throw and break things. I wanted to hit my father so hard...

Rita Ernstes is dead and you bought me a car just like the one I killed her with. Are you fucking nuts?

But, I did not say any of these things. Instead I stood very still: breathing in and out, in and out, until the fire in me passed and I could smell green grass, the scent of suburban lawns watered early. In and out, until I could see Sunday morning light spilling over the trees, casting friendly shadows down the street.

This was what my mother had been crying about: she and my father had fought over whether or not I was ready to drive again. Dad believed a new Jeep would help me forget about what had happened. It was all he knew to do.

The new Jeep was just like the old one, except that it was blue instead of yellow. It had the same black canvas top, short wheelbase, and lock-out hubs for the four-wheel drive. The only real difference was this Jeep had a back seat, a back seat with seat belts. The sight of them made me feel sick.

My dad put his arm around my shoulders and gave me a squeeze. He took my duffel bag and set it beside the Jeep. "Better put the soup in first."

When we finished packing the Jeep, my parents stood on either side of me—waiting.

"Thanks," I said, finally. To say any more would have meant crossing that empty dead land that stretched between my feelings and my life. Its distance seemed impossible, its terrain impassable. "Thanks, Dad," I repeated.

My dad handed me some cash; he always did when we parted: a ten or a twenty-dollar bill. Then we hugged, my mother wiping back tears.

"C'mon now, Cay. No tears," my father said.

It had been 3 weeks since the accident when I climbed into that brand new Jeep. To get to camp I would travel the same stretch of interstate we had driven the morning of the accident. I would pass the same fields of summer corn, but this time, I would make the trip alone.

How I made the drive that day, I will never know. Perhaps like focusing on the stained glass during the funeral, I simply focused on the act of driving. I arrived at camp as planned, a little after 11:00 AM on a Sunday morning.

As I pulled into the staff parking area, I watched the dust settle behind the Jeep. An unusual sweat ran beneath my arms and down the center of my back. I smelled a little acrid. I smelled scared. It was warm, a beautiful Sunday morning, and with the engine switched off, I could hear the sounds of camp: a soft breeze running through the alfalfa, creek water bubbling over flat stones, a horse whinnying down at the barn. The sweetest sounds, however, came from the small log chapel on the other side of the creek where my friends were attending Mass. From the open windows I could hear the pure voices of young women accompanied by their guitars, a youthful choir singing simple hymns. I started feeling cold. As glad as I was to be back at camp, I was also frightened. *How would I begin, what would I say?* All around me were the sights and sounds with which I had grown up, a place as intimate to me as any I had ever known. But I was not the same person. I was the driver, the one to blame; I felt marked in a way that could not be erased.

Sitting down by the Jeep, I waited for Mass to finish. My hands shook a little. I shoved them in my pockets. *How do I do this?* My whole body started to tremble; I felt as if I might explode. *Do they hate me?* My questions made me more agitated until I wanted to hit something. I wanted to hit something so hard that I would feel my hands break apart.

Finally, my friends filed out of the chapel and headed across the footbridge to the dining hall for breakfast. They walked in a group, young women between the ages of 16 and 23. Some were dressed in cut-off shorts and T-shirts, others in overalls or worn army fatigues and men's flannel shirts. They were all sizes and shapes: small and petite, large and big boned. Some were heavy and slow moving while others were quick like the wind. In their high schools they were cheerleaders and thespians, student council presidents and nobodies special. Some made out. Some partied with nothing more than lemonade or Co-ca-Cola. There were those who protested the war in Vietnam and those who could have cared less about politics or foreign policy. There were those who had college on their minds and those who were considering marriage or the convent. At camp we lived with all these differences. Our common love of the place and who we were when we were there bridged the difference between us. At camp we were a sisterhood: one tribe, on our own, at play.

Now the tribe was walking towards me, crossing the footbridge over the creek. Watching them stilled my body and my mind. One of the younger counselors, Sandy, gave my good friend Mary Fitz a playful shove, almost knocking her into the creek.

"You bitch!" Mary shouted playfully, shoving Sandy back. I smiled as I watched the all-too-predictable exchange. Then Chris, the cook, spotted me.

"Johnson!" she yelled. Christine Schlegel in her size 11 high-top sneakers and ever-present bandanna scarf loped to me with arms spread wide.

Grateful for her warm recognition, I stood, took a deep breath, and went to meet her and the rest of my friends.

"When did you get here?"

"A few minutes ago." My answer buzzed through the small spaces between my teeth. The group grew quiet. *What are they thinking?* I felt as if I were turning to stone as the silence spread, at first uncomfort-able, and then unbearable. A couple of junior counselors, whom I did not know, turned away mumbling something about starting breakfast. The rest of us stood in silence, until Mary spoke and broke the trance:

"You're in Cabin 'C' with us, Cath. Cathy Brake too. We can take your stuff up after breakfast."

Relief flooded me, and my whole body relaxed. *Bless you Mary Fitzgerald for making a place for me.* Tears started to push their way up from my chest into my throat. But instead of letting them come, I pretended to cough and did my best to smile.

The rest of the details of that morning are lost to me, but I imagine that I moved into our cabin quickly and helped with the typical Sunday morning chores. Before the campers arrived in the late afternoon for the next week of camp, the shower house had to be mopped with bleach water and hosed down. Toilets and sinks had to be cleaned, garbage cans emptied. Each cabin had to be swept and the mattresses beat. The large covered pavilion also had to be swept and tidied with all the leftover arts and crafts thrown out and the clothing from the previous week collected in black plastic garbage bags. In a couple of hours, thanks to tape decks blaring the music of Credence, the Allman Brothers, and Grateful Dead, camp would be transformed from what looked like a refugee processing center into a fresh-looking and wholesome place just waiting for a new group of girls, their parents, and families.

Father Schneider, to whom I promised my silence, slipped quickly away that morning, as he usually did on Sundays. He had Mass to say over at our other camp, two valleys and 40 minutes of back road driving away. I imagine Father was as glad to avoid me, as I was to avoid him. From the moment I arrived back at camp, I began to dislike him; I looked for his shortcomings, and made jokes at his expense.

"Father couldn't ride a bike, let alone a horse," I once quipped over breakfast, but no one at the table laughed. I silenced my contempt. I had no idea how angry I was, how hurt. All that would come later. At the time I just wanted to be accepted, to get along, to find my place in the world.

Working with my friend Mary, high on a wooded ridge, teaching camp-craft skills, I rarely saw Becky and Anita; they worked at the other end of camp, down at the horse barn. Of course I must have seen them at meals and at night after the kids went to bed, but the distance between us was growing. If you had asked me at the time, I would not have admitted it, but it was I who was retreating from them. I felt confused and wary, especially with Becky.

One night, walking from the dining hall towards the cabin to get something warm for the evening campfire, I noticed Becky's motorcycle parked outside the camp office. Just as I got to her bike, Becky emerged, pushing the screen door open hard so that it slammed the wall behind. Janie, the Camp Director and Becky's friend, followed immediately with her own version of screen door anger. But instead of following Becky to her bike, Janie turned the opposite direction and headed uphill to the cabins. Whatever had passed between them was finished, and both were pissed.

"Hey Beck?" It was both a greeting and a question. She didn't answer but climbed onto her bike. "What's up?" I tried again. Her usually soft face was hard set and angry, her eyes on the verge of spilling over.

"Brake and Hurley got kicked out for smoking pot."

The facts didn't explain her anger, or the reason she was straddling her bike. "Where are you going?"

Becky looked directly at me. "Conley's," was all she said.

Pat Conley was the previous director of the Ranch. She had an apartment in Indianapolis, notorious for its parties, a place where anyone from camp was welcome, where Brake and Hurley could pass the remaining weeks of summer so their folks wouldn't find out that they'd been fired.

"When will you be back?"

Becky ignored my question, switched the ignition key, and rolled the bike off its stand. Lifting herself, she stepped down hard on the kickstart. The engine roared to life.

A shudder ran through me. I wanted to reach for her arm but she was already easing forward, then with a burst the bike leapt and disappeared down the road in a rooster tail of late summer dust. *Please, Becky, don't go.*

Becky was the touchstone, the person who I looked to for reassurance, whose forgiveness I craved yet could not ask for or accept, who I both pushed away from and couldn't bear to lose. I twisted the events of that goodbye in my mind, made them into evidence that she no longer liked me. The truth is, I no longer liked me.

The summer passed. Becky came back, and left again. She and Janie were at odds over the firing of the two counselors. Meanwhile, I played my guitar at campfire, horsed around with the kids, got into water fights, and did my job. I kept the promise I had made not to talk about the accident or Rita's death. Then one afternoon up at the camp-craft site, some older girls wanted to know more.

A trio of 12-year-olds: all three, long and gangly with budding breasts and widening interests, tan and blonde—they were, each and together, the picture of young womanhood. I never saw one without the other. They egged each other on and were often at the edge of trouble: smart and sassy, repentant when caught. Staff alternately loved and hated them. They had been coming to camp since they were in first grade. We knew that they would be the next wave of counselors, and so did they.

"How long will your mouth be wired shut?" one of them asked casually as we put away the tools we'd been using.

"End of the summer," I replied.

"But it is the end of the summer," another said.

"Yah, aren't you sick of eating soup all the time?" the third chimed in, laying a bow saw into the wooden box where we stored tools.

Truthfully, I do not know how I got through that summer, but I suspect that I did it by not thinking about the accident, Rita's death, the change in my friendships, and least of all about myself. I had locked that part up until these three with their questions came knocking at the door.

"I am sick of soup, but that's what I eat."

"Can't you stick stuff between the space?"

"What space?"

"The little space that opens when you talk."

I hadn't realized that there was a growing space, millimeters perhaps, but a space nonetheless, that had been opening between my top and bottom teeth as the orthodontia wiring had loosened over the last 2 months.

"Don't you have anyplace else to go?" I said, feeling trapped by their questions. I pulled my knife from its sheath and cut away some lashing that had rotted on our lean-to. When girls came to camp-craft, they slept out under the stars or under a large lean-to we had built for when it rained.

"Nah, we've got a free period," Jenny, the oldest of the three, answered.

I hacked at the old lashing, trying to free it as much as I longed to be free of them.

"How did you break your jaw, anyway?"

Jenny's question may have been innocent, but I was sure that everyone knew what had happened. I slashed hard at a piece of rotten rope still bound to its pole. The knife missed, bounced off the wood, and glanced against my other hand. I didn't feel the cut until the blood started running.

"Whoa, shit!" Jenny stepped back then forward. "Are you OK?"

Grabbing a bandanna from my back pocket, I pressed it against my hand and whirled to face the girls.

"If you're on a fucking free period, then go and do it somewhere else."

The fire in my voice scorched their faces; they reddened, and one by one turned to go. Jenny was the last. Her look was one of confusion and hurt. There was a part of me that was deeply wounded and who wanted to be seen, but that part was also fiercely guarded. Jenny had provoked the guardian.

A few evenings later we were lining up for dinner outside the dining hall. The grass was turning brown, the creek running low; summer was just about over. Looking at the growing column of girls, I saw the triumvirate laughing and playing a game of hand slap. Two players face each other. One holds her hands out, palms up. The other places her hands, palms down, lightly above the open hands below. The player whose hands are on the bottom tries to flip them over and catch or slap the hands of the one above. It requires quick reflexes and the ability to veil your intent to move. Jenny was an ace. I walked back along the line to where they stood.

"Hey," I said, "I'm sorry about the other day." They stopped and turned to face me. It seemed they were waiting for something more, an excuse or reason. I did not give them one, still guarding the gate. Instead, I turned and walked back to the front of the line where the senior staff gathered.

The camp's dining hall was a low, long, cinderblock building painted white with dark green roof and dark green trim. Inside, the same: even the picnic tables were painted white. A large fireplace anchored one end of the building. At the other end stood a screen door that snapped back on its spring with a loud bang whenever anyone exited.

Dinner that particular night consisted of government subsidy meatloaf, mashed potatoes, and green peas. While I did not miss the opportunity to eat the meatloaf, I did long for something green. Mary was sitting next to me with a little mountain of peas resting on her tin tray, a mountain that called to me like a siren. Someone must have noticed the way I was gazing at Mary's peas, while sucking my usual quart of potato soup from a glass jar.

"Man, Johnson, you look pathetic. When do you get to eat again?"

The din in the dining hall had risen to its typical level, which seemed several decibels above that of a rock concert: everyone yelling to be heard.

I looked up. In my mind it is Becky asking the question. Becky inviting back another part of me. Becky, with eyes lost in her smile, acting normal with me at the end of summer when nothing had been normal between us for months.

Sitting up very tall, I ceremoniously reached over and lifted the top pea from Mary's tray. Gingerly I rotated that soft green bead between my thumb and forefinger. Then, with great mock effort, I climbed out from the table and stood at my place, holding the pea in front of me. A soft chant began to rise above the din: "Johnson, Johnson, Johnson..." I climbed up on the bench, standing nearly 6 feet above the table and all my friends. Still holding the pea in front of me. The chant grew— all eyes now on me. I raised the pea to heaven, and then as the chanting grew even louder, did my best to open my mouth. Straining against the orthodontic wires and surgical pins, I found the small space between my teeth, the one Jenny had noticed. Placing the pea against that space, I paused. I understood the importance of a dramatic moment. Without further hesitation, I wedged and smashed the pea through the tiny opening. Then, I lifted my hand as if to say *wait, there's more*. The dining hall fell into silence. I held the pea in my mouth and closed my eyes to savor its taste: fresh, green, and buttery. I rolled it around with my tongue a couple of times, feeling it dissolve. Finally, I swallowed it with a gulp loud enough to be heard at the back of the room. The dining hall erupted in cheers and applause. I lowered my hand and grinned in a way that I hadn't all summer. Then, taking my bow, I returned to my soup. My friends laughed, slapping me and each other on the back in delight.

That night, lying in my bunk, I listened to the hum of the cicadas, the small rhythm of even breathing, of the cabin asleep. I felt the softness of the sheet that covered me, the length of me in my bunk, the sag of the metal springs beneath my weight. It was as if eating that pea had been another small threshold, like recognizing the straw beside me. I did not feel proud or excited, relieved or hopeful. But I did feel content.

For years I honestly believed that the accident had broken and scattered my heart into little pieces, many of which would never be recovered. I can see now that it was my own doing. I kept parts of my heart hidden as a way of protecting myself from feeling too much—too much anger, too much sadness, too much of anything. I believed that I should do as much as I could to make up for what I had done. Even feeling content, when I thought about it, seemed somehow wrong.

In a matter of days, camp was over. I went back to Indianapolis, packed for school, and finally got my mouth unwired. One would think that I would have had a lot to say. But the promise I had made had become a practice, like second nature. A few weeks later, I moved 2100 miles from home and began living in a college dorm, going to classes, and quietly getting on with life.

PART II

LESSONS IN THE WILDERNESS

"If you can't think and coil a rope at the same time, Johnson, you're hopeless." My professor gave me a playful slap on the shoulder as I worked the kinks out of 150 feet of Goldline rope.

Now in my second year at The Evergreen State College, in Olympia, Washington, I was studying outdoor education. On that particular November afternoon, our classroom had been a granite cliff overlooking a long, narrow lake in the shadow of the Olympic Mountains. The day had been overcast though dry. A stiff wind had made for cold hands while moments of sunlight piercing the clouds like a silver lance had made for stunning views. We were a small group practicing mountain rescue techniques, and as my professor watched me haul up an arm's length of rope and lay it in my open palm, he simultaneously engaged me in a philosophical conversation about risk and leadership in the outdoors.

"So," he posed, squinting his eyes at me and stroking his bearded chin, "how much risk is acceptable?"

Dr. William F. Unsoeld, known to everyone simply as Willi, was a larger-than-life figure: a famous mountaineer and philosopher, one of Evergreen's founding faculty and a beloved mentor to many. When I met Willi he was in his late forties, though he looked older. The years spent climbing, especially those at high altitude, had taken their toll.

His face was etched with deep craggy lines, his hawk-like nose burned so many times it appeared permanently pink and peeling. And yet, there was nothing old about Willi. When he headed across campus, he did not walk but strode with his legs pumping like pistons and arms swinging. He had a voice that boomed out of his chest and in the classroom he fired questions like cannon shots. The first time he addressed me, I was so startled by the blast that I nearly fell out of my chair. But like so many others, I adored Willi. He was a man wildly alive and fiercely determined, a man who believed in wilderness both for the preservation of spirit and the sharpening of character. Any chance that Willi got, he would leave the confines of the classroom and take his students outside.

I hauled up another arm's length of rope and responded to the question Willi had posed.

"There's no way to remove all the risk," I said, "but it is our job as guides to make a trip as safe as possible."

"That's true!" Willi said enthusiastically, and then reducing his voice to a stage whisper, "But, not the right answer; the right answer is..." voice booming now, "No amount of risk is acceptable!" He continued, "That's what parents expect when they entrust their kids to you. They expect those kids to come back whole. But, it's the very risk of death that creates the experience that the kids are longing for, that brings about the change their parents hope to see."

With little conscious intent, I had chosen a professional path that would place me, time and again, in a position of responsibility for the lives of others. I, who believed she had made a grave mistake, an error of judgment that had cost the life of a friend, would spend years guiding others in situations and environments that placed our lives at risk. And, if the choice of a teacher was less than conscious on my part, Willi Unsoeld could not have been more perfect for the job.

Willi talked openly about death and its place in life. Something I needed to learn. He had lost plenty of friends to the mountains. One day he would lose his own daughter, Devi, on a climb together in the

Himalaya, on the very mountain for which she had been named. After that tragedy, when he lectured, Willi would often ask,

"How do you handle death?"

He would allow the question to hang in the expectant air, until the silence grew uncomfortable. Then he would answer in a voice softened by grief. "You don't. You don't handle death. Death handles you."

With a doctorate in philosophy, Willi Unsoeld understood the subject of death intimately. He'd written of it, read of it, and debated it openly. With the death of his daughter, he lived it. Although I never told him my own story, when I was with him the weight of it seemed less. By coming to the Northwest, I had embarked on a journey, a search for self-acceptance, forgiveness, and faith. Willi was my first guide.

"You're not twisting your wrist enough," Willi said. "Wow, you've got a mess of rope there; better start over."

Turning, I faced him, not wanting to believe what I had heard.

"You really want me to start over again?" Immediately, I wished I hadn't asked. I knew better; the coils of rope in my hand hung in various shapes: a few loose and near perfect, others twisting into stiff figure eights. A mountaineering rope is a lifeline. Among climbers it is treated with reverence, a reverence most flatlanders do not understand. Standing with Willi on the edge of that cliff in the November afternoon light, I knew that he was absolutely serious about me starting over; I also knew he would stand there until I got it right.

Willi was a tough and loving father figure, one so different from my own. My father, so often fearful in the face of difficulty, was overcome by that which he could not control. And, while he required obedience, my father expected little else from me. He was proud of my accomplishments but never pushed me to do more. Willi, on the other hand, challenged, cajoled, and called forth in his students a radiance of heart and a toughness of mind. He always wanted us to do better. Although

I did not like making mistakes, I felt lucky to be on the receiving end of his exacting standards.

"Rope," I yelled and heaved the tangled coil out into the late afternoon air. The sun struck the golden skein as it loosened and fell out of sight. Then, everything became quiet. The quiet grew large. Time stood still. The long shadows and yellow light spread across the land. I took a deep breath. The air tasted of cedar and sparkled like fine crystal. I forgot my frustration over the task at hand, forgot Willi at my side. I forgot everything. There was only the air's moist coolness, the rock's gritty hardness, and the forest's sweet and pungent scent. For a few moments, I was nothing more than wind, wood, and stone.

All the great mystical traditions speak of the omnipotent present. Some find it through meditation or prayer, others in nature or a moment of pure awareness. When it happened that day, I had a clear, albeit fleeting, sense that everything was right in the world, that all things arise out of one source, that everything is both temporary and eternal. In that knowing there was no more searching, no more longing, and no more loss.

I took another breath and became aware of myself breathing, aware of the rope and Willi waiting. Pulling up an arm's length of rope, I twisted it and laid it in the palm of my hand. Arm length by arm length, up came the rope, each coil hanging perfectly, round and loose, in my grip. I smiled, and as if on cue, Willi started in again.

"So, you think you're ready, Johnson? You think you can teach your students enough skill and good judgment so that they can travel through the wilderness on their own, without you?"

I didn't know if I was ready, but I knew that if I could learn to tap that place where everything was right—I would be fine.

A few months later I drove out of Olympia on a cold, wet February morning, remembering Willi's question. "Do you think you're ready?"

I had not planned to make a cross-country trip in the middle of winter, in the middle of an academic quarter, but when I received a telephone call from the Minnesota Outward Bound School informing me they would grant me a job interview, I leapt at the chance.

Perhaps I heard what I wanted to hear, when my own Outward Bound instructor, 4 years earlier, had encouraged me by saying I would make a good instructor, that I was a "natural." From that moment onward, I dreamed of working for the Minnesota Outward Bound School. I worked hard to realize that dream. Each summer before or after camp, I traveled back to the Boundary Waters for canoe trips. I spent weekends teaching my friends to rock climb on the small limestone cliffs of Illinois and Ohio using a well-thumbed copy of *Mountaineering: Freedom of the Hills*. It was that dream that helped me move on after the accident, that carried me away from Indiana, to the Pacific Northwest and college at Evergreen; all of it had been in order to be an Outward Bound instructor. As I left Olympia on that February morning, I was excited, restless, eager, and anxious thinking that my dream was about to come true.

Driving out of Seattle east on Interstate 90, I wound my way up Snoqualmie Pass. I had spent the last 2 years, my freshman and sophomore years in college, studying outdoor education. Willi had encouraged me to apply for the Outward Bound position even though I was not yet 21. He knew of my desire to instruct and he knew my skills. He also sensed in me an intense need to be attached to something, to find a place to land. Since leaving Indiana, I only circled people and places, dropping in but never really settling. When invited to events or parties, I usually only stayed a short time. I always felt scared to be noticed and avoided the kinds of conversations that required much more than pleasantries or simple opinions. I had constructed a façade, that of a strong, competent, and independent woman. Yet I knew just how brittle the façade was and believed that if I allowed anyone to get too close, it would crumble.

A few miles below Snoqualmie Pass, I entered winter's world of black and white. Banks of icy snow lined the road. Douglas firs stood in silhouette with a fresh dusting of gray powder. It was a cold and unwelcoming sight. It reflected the part of me who felt inconsolable and alone.

As the Jeep labored upward, I downshifted gears often from third into second. Revving the engine and building up speed, I would then shift back up. It was the same inside of me; I constantly kept shifting away from my feelings, relying instead on that part of me who knew how to stay busy and get things done.

When I crossed over the summit, I joined a line of tractor-trailers descending into the open farmlands of eastern Washington. As our caravan found its way out of the mountains, we found our way into a new day as well. It was a bright morning with blue sky and sun. I put on my sunglasses, then found a scratchy station out of Ellensburg playing old Bob Wills tunes; it was good to be on the road.

Taking to the road comes naturally to me. My father was a traveling salesman who put 90,000 miles a year on his car, covering a four-state territory. His products were items that supplied the big three automakers in Detroit, bushings and bearings, the stuff of door hinges and engine mounts. There were always one or two small boxes of steel parts, samples for his sales calls, in the trunk of his car, a car that was always American and always a convertible.

I cannot think of my life without thinking of cars and driving. I can remember most of the cars we had when I was growing up, their make, model, and details. A large part of my childhood was spent in a car: riding with my dad on business, taking trips with my mom and him, or hanging out with friends just driving. Even after the accident, I still loved to drive.

For most of my childhood, my father would leave early on Monday morning to *go on the road*. That was how we referred to his work. My mother would kiss him longer than usual and then she and I would stand in the driveway, waving as he drove off. A couple of days would pass and it would be *just us girls*, she and I. Together, my mother and I were relaxed and easygoing but a bit aimless as well. My father was the center of our lives, the demanding and charming sun around which she and I, like two moons, orbited. On the day that my father was to return home each week, my mother and I would bathe early, using bubbles and perfume. We would dress up in front of her big closet mirror and then run into his arms when he climbed from his car. As I grew older, the details of the ritual changed. I dressed up for him less and less, but the welcoming essence of it remained.

After I left home, my folks continued to live their lives with cars and driving as an integral component. Years later while driving to the airport with my mother at the end of a visit to Indianapolis, she told me a story that showed just how little had changed for the two of them in this regard.

Mom and I were riding in the air-conditioned comfort of her champagne-colored Mercedes. I drove while she kept up a running commentary about the changes that the city had undergone over the 20 years since I had moved away.

"See? Over there." My mother jabbed her finger against the window glass, her artificial nails tapping an urgent Morse code to get my attention.

"Where?"

"Over there, the liquor store." She tapped the window harder.

Glancing in her direction, I saw a large corner parking lot surrounded by chainlink fence. The cement lay in broken slabs, tall weeds pushing up through the cracks. At the back of the lot stood a windowless cinderblock building. On top, a red neon sign identified the place: Discount Liquors, the word *discount* flashing while *liquors* stayed lit.

"What about the liquor store?" I asked.

"That's where your father and I play our cards."

"Cards?"

"Yes, right there." More finger jabs on the window. "We play our cards and then drive across the street and get our hot dogs."

Across from the Discount Liquor store is another cinderblock building. But this one has plate glass window in the front with "Nick's" painted in a large arc of bright yellow letters, letters outlined in red to add depth. At the edge of Nick's parking lot is a square yellow sign that turns faithfully on the axis of a tall pole and reads: Nick's Dogs and Chili.

"You play cards in a liquor store parking lot and then drive across the street to buy hot dogs?" I am incredulous.

"Uh-huh." She nods, her lips pursed in a slight smile. She knows I cannot fathom this as interesting, intimate, or fun.

During their retirement years, Bill and Cay performed the same routine daily. They would attend noon Mass and then drive to one of several, vacant, trash-strewn parking lots for a card game. The parking lots were located close to a favorite lunch stop. The lunch stops were usually dark taverns or greasy diners located in industrial neighborhoods. One had navy bean soup my father loved, another a Reuben sandwich piled high with sauerkraut, which was my mother's favorite, and then there was Nick's. Also, a cooler was always packed so that they could have a cocktail with their card game, their car transformed into a living room on wheels. And with cards to play, they never cared about the view.

After crossing the Idaho state line, I stopped for a late breakfast in a café on Lake Coeur d'Alene. The lake had not frozen completely over but was rimmed in ice and surrounded in winter white.

When making a long drive, I often pass the time by imagining what life is like in the towns through which I travel. I like reading the headlines in the rural papers and listening in on conversations at nearby tables in diners and cafés. Just that morning in Coeur d'Alene, a young family: a mom, dad, and three kids, who looked to be between the ages of 2 and 6, were talking about their summer vacation plans.

"When we go to Disneyland," the oldest one said, "we'll stay in a hotel."

"That's right, sweetheart. Eat your pancake. Honey, help the baby."

The mother responded to the boy, helped her daughter cut her pancakes into bite-size pieces, and directed her husband who was reading the sports page while supposedly feeding their toddler who pushed his food across the shiny stainless surface of the high chair onto the floor. The mother looked to be my age but her life seemed as foreign to me as if she were from another country. In some ways rural America is another country. Conservative values, Republican ideals, high school football, hard work, and church attendance mark the lives of many who inhabit our country's small towns. Being from Indiana, I understand this point of view; I grew up surrounded by it. It never really fit, though. I never saw things in black and white and the older I grew, the more aware I became that there was another world beyond my small Midwestern one—one of art, beauty, politics, philosophic conversation, and spiritual knowledge that I wanted to explore.

If Interstate 90 flies across Idaho, it stretches out for a day and a half across Montana. In early February, western Montana laid snow covered and wind scoured in every direction. By late afternoon, a heavy ceiling of clouds lowered over the land and I no longer needed sunglasses. The road grew monotonous; I saw few cars and the same trucks kept passing me, our fuel stops creating a game of leapfrog between us. Mountains were always in the distance, either before me or behind me. Thankfully, the road was dry and I planned to make it to Billings before I stopped for the night.

A long drive gives a person plenty of time to think. It would seem only natural that the accident would come to mind, but it didn't. I had buried it deep. And, although it haunted me, I rarely thought about it directly.

Just outside of Billings, I found a small, friendly-looking motel, one story, with ten units. There were a couple of large pickup trucks parked in the lot and a nice woman behind the desk.

"You travelin' alone?" she asked, looking at my registration.

I nodded.

I wondered what she was thinking: was she thinking about the weather, what might happen if I got caught in a snow storm; the fact that I was a woman traveling alone; maybe she was simply asking to make sure I didn't have anyone else waiting in the car. She handed me a key.

"Number 8," she said, nodding towards the night.

After opening the door of unit #8, I fumbled for a light switch. An overhead fixture with a single 60-watt bulb lit the room. It was a dingy place, smelling of stale cigarette smoke, pine scented disinfectant, and creosote. The creosote smell came from an exposed beam overhead that was black and tarry, as if it had had former life as an electric light pole or railroad tie. "What do you expect for $26?" I said, immediately feeling self-conscious, the sound of my voice loud in the silence of the night. It was late and cold. I knew I should get to bed, but I felt uneasy. Tossing my pack on the bed, I went over and turned the heat up to high, my breath making little clouds as I breathed. Then I wandered about the small space looking for more light, looking for a way to brighten both the room and my mood. I turned on the TV, switched on a small fluorescent light in the bathroom, and then turned on the one lamp beside the bed. Finally the room seemed inhabitable, except for the cold. The fan on the heater roared, but did not take away the chill. I kept going over to the vent and holding out my hand to see if the air blowing out was hot. At best it was barely warm. Convinced the heat was not going to improve, I crawled into bed wearing all my clothes and fell asleep with the TV and the lights still on.

Following the accident, it would have been understandable if I had felt afraid to drive. Instead, I placed that fear on flying. Whenever I flew, it felt like a 500-pound block was sitting on my chest. For years I had a recurring dream: I would board a plane, buckle my seat belt, and know the flight would end in a crash. In the dream, I know that I will survive but must go through the whole horrible, helpless ordeal. I look anxiously at my fellow passengers, wondering who will be injured, who killed? The plane takes off, then we begin losing altitude, people scream, and I wait, gripping the arms of my seat for the terrible impact. When it finally comes, I wake up breathing hard and sweating, forearms shaking. I dreamed that dream with little variation for years. When I actually did fly, I often took medication to stay calm.

I also hated being surprised or disoriented by the dark or unfamiliar surroundings. When I camped, I preferred tarps over tents; I could more easily see what was around me and get out if I needed. Inside, when I was alone, I often slept with the lights on and sometimes the radio or TV as well. I felt embarrassed about all of this; such fearfulness did not fit the persona of a competent and strong outdoorswoman, but I also felt utterly helpless to change it. That night outside of Billings was simply another lights-and-TV-on kind of night.

The next morning dawned bright and icy cold. The engine turned over sluggishly and the freezing air seeped through my parka, pack boots, and fleece-lined gloves. Even the coffee in the thermos stayed hot for only a couple of hours. As I drove, I distracted myself from the cold by fantasizing about the coming summer when I would be instructing for Outward Bound. I pictured teaching knots, portaging canoes, encouraging students down rappels, and hearing the sound of loons as the lakes disappeared into the evening mist. I once read that if you can truly see yourself doing something, you have a better chance of doing it. So, all the way across eastern Montana through South Dakota to the Minnesota state line, I remembered my favorite lakes, fishing spots, the hard portages and the easy put-ins. I believed I knew the Boundary Waters and the Quetico well, having led four of my own trips there in the years since I was first introduced to the area as an Outward Bound student. This was another plus in my favor, I thought, feeling confident that I would get the job. I had a recommendation from Willi Unsoeld, who had helped bring Outward Bound to the United States. I was an alumna of the Minnesota school and had been studying outdoor education for 2 years in college. In addition, I was American Red Cross certified in Water Safety Instruction and Advanced First Aid. What other credentials could I possibly need?

So busy was I imagining my future and listing my qualifications that I barely noticed crossing the Missouri River. Before I knew it, I was outside of Bemidji, where I planned to stay the night. I found a slightly better motel; there was an older couple next door to me with whom I struck up a conversation. That night I felt secure and slept soundly in the dark, with only the glow from the motel's sign like a night light outside the window.

The next morning I arrived on time at the Minnesota Outward Bound School offices. I met Derek Pritchard, the school's director, who ushered me into his office for our interview. He asked me about my background, and how Willi was doing. He told me they had climbed together in the Tetons. I found Derek's British accent charming, but he was also cool in his welcome, very business-like. After his initial questions, Derek gave me some hypothetical situations to problem solve and seemed satisfied with my answers. He sat back, looked out the window to the train yards, then across the desk at me. I knew he was deciding something and I felt anxious.

"You're too young."

I wasn't sure that I heard what he said.

"Excuse me?"

"You are too young. The minimum age for instructors is 21, you are only 20. I can't hire you."

My face flushed. A knot lodged in my throat. *Why the interview if I was never eligible in the first place?* I looked at Derek without blinking. He continued to say a few more things but I stopped listening, unable to believe what was happening. He rose from his desk smiling, a better-luck-next-time kind of smile, then extended his hand. I took it. We shook. I reached for my parka and left. At the street, sound returned: cars driving by, studded tires rolling rough over patches of bare pavement, a train moving through the yard, somewhere the hammering and banging sounds of new construction, and then, the noon whistle at a nearby factory. "Time for lunch," I said sarcastically, but I was not hungry. I walked to the Jeep and found a parking ticket on the windshield. *Fuck! What the fuck else?* I wadded the paper up, tossed it hard onto the street, and drove away.

"Just like that..." I said out loud to no one. I had driven 1500 miles in the middle of winter, for a 45-minute interview whose outcome had previously been decided by the year of my birth before I ever said a word. Furious, I drove out of Duluth swearing like a trucker. I flipped off anyone who passed me, and said "fuck" in every conceivable combination until I wore myself out, the fire abated, and the stars shone. Somewhere in South Dakota, I stopped feeling angry and just felt tired.

I slept in a truck stop that night, curled in my sleeping bag in the back seat of the Jeep. The next 2 days I drove the rest of the way home, flattened.

Everyone was very conciliatory and supportive when I returned to Olympia. None of it helped. I walked through my days in a state of perpetual moping until Willi confronted me.

I had gone to his office for my winter quarter academic evaluation meeting. After the perfunctory exchange of opinions about my studies, he pushed the papers aside, sat forward in his chair, and asked:

"So what about instructing?"

"Not old enough."

"Not the right answer."

"What is the right answer then?"

"You tell me."

I cursed under my breath, tired of coming up with the right answers. This was not a philosophical discussion for me.

"So, you're giving up?" Willi said.

"No."

"Then what?"

"I don't know. I don't know what to do next."

"Get on with the dream. Line up something for this summer that will give you more experience and hone your skills. Unless," he paused, "you really don't think you can do it." A few seconds passed before he said, "Maybe you can't."

"That's not true," I said hotly. "I will be a damn good instructor. You know it and I know it." I glared at him, my heart pounding. He looked back just as hard. Then a quiet settled in me. I could feel it and he could see it.

"Right answer," Willi said. "That's the right answer, Cath."

I carry a strong stubborn streak. Telling me I can't do something often ignites in me a fire to prove the judgment wrong. *If not this year Derek Pritchard, then next.* For the remainder of that year, I kept my sights re-focused on instructing for Outward Bound.

If I felt determined to make the Outward Bound dream come true, I also felt pulled forward towards it. My path was not necessarily logical or linear, but it did seem guided. That summer I ended up teaching swimming to native children in the Pribilof Islands of Alaska. I learned about being a minority, about earning the respect and trust of the native community. I witnessed the slaughter of the North American fur seal, so necessary to the traditions and economies of the villages, so against my own environmental ethics and beliefs. It was a summer that matured me, widened my view, and gave me a new capacity for facing complex and conflicted situations with greater openness and willingness to listen and learn.

The following year I reached the magic age of 21 and was immediately hired by Outward Bound. Not by the Minnesota School though, but by the North Carolina School. The summer of 1976, instead of heading for the Boundary Waters, I headed into the Southern Appalachian Mountains as if it were meant to be. I would spend the rest of my twenties in those mountains, living close to the earth, walking instead of driving, and eating way too much oatmeal which, true to Rita Pougiales' prediction, I never burned. I derived a deep satisfaction from introducing others to the harsh and delicate beauties of the wild, the exhilaration of its summits, fast rivers, and deep caves, the peace of creeks, forests, and meadows studded in wildflowers. There were plenty of times, too, when I would wait as a student questioned her or his ability to go on, waited with a compassion born from my own experience. Each of us carries our own right answer and we know it when we hear it.

North Carolina Outward Bound

Throughout the 1970s, I shuttled back and forth between winters in the Pacific Northwest, where I attended college, to summers in North Carolina, where I instructed for Outward Bound. I kept the winter months interesting by transferring to a small Lutheran college, enrolling in a nursing program, and learning to row. I had no need to keep summer interesting; working for the North Carolina Outward Bound School (NCOBS) was everything I wanted.

I was teaching young people about wilderness travel and more importantly, about themselves. Perhaps the old adage *we teach what we most need to learn* applied to me. Each June as I drove across the country, and finally up the 14 miles of rutted, gravel road that led into the green forested and gray, granite mountains of the Southern Appalachians, I felt increasingly happy and more alive.

By my second summer at NCOBS, I was practically an old-timer. I knew which expedition routes were more remote, which promised stunning views and which rugged hiking. My maps were dog-eared and heavily marked: an "X" for a deep green swimming hole, a craggy summit, a *holler* where interesting mountain folk lived, an abandoned field where a hungry crew could dig for volunteer potatoes or find early apples in forgotten trees. That second summer, 1976, my life seemed to be falling into place. There was only one exception: I had yet to fall in love.

It was mid-July and my crew was in base camp for a few days. I was looking forward to spending the night away from them, being with other staff, and especially to seeing Susan, the woman with whom I shared a tarp. Like me, Susan also spent her winters as a college student, and for the last 2 years we had been housemates in Washington, tarp mates in North Carolina.

When I left my crew, they were washing their dinner pots by headlamp. A gibbous moon lit my way as I walked along a winding path that led from their camp along the creek to Susan's and my tarp nestled uphill next to a house-size boulder not far from the base camp's climbing area. As I walked, the crickets droned. The air was warm, scented with summer's perfume. I hurried my steps, excited to see Susan after a week out on expedition. When my path started climbing more steeply, I knew I was getting close. Up slope the woods were deeper, the moon barely reaching through. I used my feet and my other senses to make up for what my eyes could no longer see. *Won't be long now.* Then the big stone that hid our tarp came into black shape before me. *Home,* I thought happily.

Lighting the candle Susan and I kept beside the tarp, I smiled appreciating the comfort of a simple light in the velvet dark. *Where is she?* I wondered as I took off my boots and crawled under the clear plastic sheeting pitched like a tent between two large maples. As I waited for Susan, I pondered how I had come to know her.

Over the years I had been attracted to different men, but when it came to anything beyond kissing, I would grow cold both to the kisses and the relationship. It was women I enjoyed being with, women I admired. After 2 years of college at Evergreen, I knew about women's music, about lesbian and gay rights—yet I still did not, or would not, see how these applied to me. And although I kept living in houses full of women, sharing beds platonically with them, I kept waiting for a man to ignite something more than likeable curiosity in my heart.

Burnell had become a good friend, a climbing partner, and a study mate during my second year at Evergreen. Tall and sinewy with a wild head of dark curly hair that he managed with bandannas and wool hats, he had become a regular fixture in our house of women. During the winter of 1975 we studied calculus, the mountains, and life together.

"Hey there," he said, coming through the front door, which banged in the wind. I went to close it as he shed his backpack and rain parka, soaked from the 4-mile bike ride from the college fire station where he lived to our house on the west side of town.

"What do you have in there?" I asked as he pulled a loaf of bread from his pack.

"Sourdough, fresh from the oven." He gently untied the plastic bag and pulled a perfect loaf from it that filled the room with the smell of homemade bread. Placing it on the table, he gave me a warm hug.

"Sue made chili; it's heating on the stove."

"Where are those two?"

He was referring to my roommates, the two Sues: Susan Wanser and Sue Stadler, both Evergreen students who, like me, spent summers instructing for Outward Bound.

"Wanser is down at the organic farm and Sue is up visiting her folks in Seattle."

"We have the place to ourselves?"

"For the evening."

1954 Division Street was a run-down student rental with peeling yellow paint and a sagging porch. Poised precariously on a busy corner, the house had once been a gas station; the covered island that had held the pumps still stood out front. I thought this added character to an otherwise dilapidated structure. With little more than a nod and a handshake, the house had been ours for $300 a month, a bargain in a college town where students actively competed for off-campus housing. Inside the front door that, depending on the weather, either swung open on its own accord or needed a shoulder shove to free it from the jamb, was a long living room. Weighted by a wood stove at one end and a bay window at the other, it was the house's best feature. In addition, there were two small bedrooms, a bathroom with cracked pink linoleum that had faded to a gray-fleshy color, and a narrow kitchen some previous tenant had painted turquoise blue.

After dinner, Burnell and I sat on the sofa working calculus problems. The ideas came easy to Burnell, much harder for me.

"I hate this," I said, closing my book exasperated.

"It's a different language, that's all; once you understand its rules, it's easier." Burnell slid over next to me and kissed me on the cheek.

All fall we had been growing closer. We studied together more and more, took moonlit walks to the campus beach. Slowly we found ourselves holding hands walking in the forest, along the road beside the water. Somewhere along the line we started kissing each other goodnight. Those kisses were tentative and soft.

"Hey," he said softly, turning my shoulders towards him. "You'll get it." He eased me back on the couch and gently climbed on top. Kissing my face with the lightest brush of lips, his hair fell onto my face. I kissed his neck as he lowered himself onto me. This was my dear friend with whom I felt at home and unafraid. We kissed some more. I could feel his arms tightening, his breathing grow deeper, then could feel his heat, and before long his hardness. While I could feel all this in him, I couldn't feel anything within me—no hunger, no heat, no desire.

"I can't," I finally said, squirming out from beneath him.

He kissed me again.

"Please. Don't." I sat up and moved away from him on the couch.

I don't remember what we said to each other next, just the emptiness that settled in me after he closed the door and rode away into the rain-driven night. I knew that I had failed at something elemental. A man I really liked, I couldn't love. A few days later, we walked to the beach and talked.

"Cath," he said, "maybe you're a lesbian. You live with women. Are you in love with either of them?"

"I'm not a lesbian," I said emphatically. "And I am not in love with my roommates."

How perceptive he had been. I was madly in love with women. Becky had been the first. I had crushes on both my roommates and cuddled up contentedly with them on cold nights. But still I could not admit it—that I was gay.

Burnell was a gentle soul, a good man and a good friend. After that evening though, our friendship changed. We spent less and less time together. Eventually, I noticed that he seemed to spend an increasing amount of time with another woman. I felt disappointed and also relieved. Still I could not have explained why. I felt as if I had lost something, something I never possessed. At the same time, I no longer had to question myself or feel badly that I could not meet his sweet advances.

Back under the tarp, the crickets grew loud and a little wind stirred through the forest, flickering the candle. I tried writing in my journal but could not seem to concentrate. *Where is she?* I wondered again. Finally, tiredness got the better of me and I shed my sweater, shirt, and grungy shorts and climbed into my sleeping bag. It was then that I noticed a folded note on top of Susan's bag.

Cath, am staying the night with Mike, see you tomorrow. S.

I smiled, recognizing her handwriting. Mike was another staff member, a mutual friend. Nothing seemed odd, except that a slow sick feeling was spreading up from my stomach and lodging in my throat. A woman knows when she's been left no matter how innocent the circumstances, or how much she wants to believe otherwise. I reassured myself that this was nothing, but the longer I lay there trying to sleep, the more agitated I felt. A new question began inside me: *How could she do this?* It was the question that made no sense. How could she do what—spend the night with a man, a friend—what was wrong with that? Nothing, except that it was me that she had spent the night with for the better part of 2 years. The wind came up and with it the smell of rain. Eventually, I slept and by morning we were finished.

Susan and Mike were seeing each other; she moved her things from our tarp to his tent and I hated her for it. Yet, I wrestled with my reaction.

"I've waited for almost 2 years," she said when we finally talked. She sounded hurt and angry. "I waited for you to get it, but you just don't. I wanted you as a lover, not a friend."

Her words stung, and they were true. Maybe if I had agreed, admitted she was right, she would have returned. I will never know. What I do know is that I was morose for days, walking through the rest of my course like a zombie. And when it was over, I went off and got drunk. I wanted her to come and rescue me, but she never did. The days passed and we began to prepare for the next course. Whenever I saw her, I smoldered with hurt and refused to speak. When I saw her with Mike, I had to turn and leave; she seemed impossibly happy. At night I cried until I slept: I hated her, I hated him, but mostly I hated me.

Five days passed like 500, but finally the next course started. I thought I would feel better; I did not. Instead, I was distracted. I did not care about my students or their experience, only the pain I was feeling. As the crew struggled to gel, they fought with each other constantly and on their final expedition, they broke the most important rule of the experience: they split up. Half of the group made their way out of the woods to a paved road and hitchhiked to a public campground; they passed their expedition days swimming in a big lake, bumming beers from other campers, and then hitching back to the school in order to arrive back on schedule. When they walked into camp, they pretended they had been hiking all the while. Meanwhile, the other half completed their expedition following the route as planned. They arrived exhausted, dirty, and mad. Sorting out what happened between the two groups, all the feelings the split had engendered and the lessons both had learned, kept us up late, very late, for two nights in a row. While the rest of the school celebrated the end of the course, our crew continued to process angrily. Facilitating these long and painful conversations was difficult and in the end little was settled, let alone healed. All twelve students left hurt, believing that they had been cheated in some way. And, in some way they had been. While their lack of cohesion was not my fault, their behavior reflected my lack of attention to them from the start. Even though I knew this, I felt I had failed.

As soon as the post-course work was complete, I left the base camp, alone, again. This time I did not get drunk, but sought refuge from the one place I thought I could go—Nancy Phifer's house.

Nancy lived on the top floor of an old Victorian house in the town of Morganton, North Carolina. At that time some 15,000 people lived in Morganton, most of them employed by the government. The state school for the deaf, a large veterans hospital, a medium-size correctional facility, and the state mental institution were all located in this sleepy town at the eastern edge of the Appalachian Mountains. Nancy worked as a social worker. She was fair and freckled, tall and slender, with long and unruly brown hair that was showing its first signs of gray. She also was the only person I had ever met who wore pink-framed glasses. Nancy was a quiet and thoughtful person whose dry sense of humor leaked out, to my thinking, in just the right moments. I met Nancy when I became friends with those in her circle. I felt a rare sense of ease with her. Looking back, I can see how guarded I was with people then and how unusual it was to meet someone with whom I lowered that guard, with whom I could be vulnerable.

Walking up the stairs to Nancy's apartment, I felt utterly worn out. Each step presented an invitation to turn around, but where would I go? When I finally knocked on her door, I prayed both that she would answer and that she would not be home.

"Hey, Cath," she said. "What are you doin' here?" After the question, Nancy paused and looked at me a little harder. "Are you alright?"

"Can I stay the night?"

I remember nothing of what happened next, nothing that was said. I only remember how fresh the clean sheets on her guest bed smelled when I climbed beneath them. I slept for 18 hours. Later Nancy told me that she had felt so concerned at one point, she almost called a doctor friend for reassurance. When I awoke it was evening. Nancy brought me a bath towel and tilted her head in the direction of the bathroom.

"When you're finished, come on out to the kitchen. I'll have something for you to eat."

We sat in silence at the kitchen table. I picked at the salad she had made, sipping iced tea from a tall green glass. Nancy sat across from me, waiting without placing that waiting upon me. I was holding onto what I had to say. Maybe I knew that if I spoke, what I would say would be true and everything would be different. Finally, I let go.

"Nancy?"

"Uh-huh?"

Getting the words out felt impossible. I kept willing them up only to feel them fall back down inside me. Nancy must have sensed my struggle.

"Cath, did something happen on your course?"

"No. Well, sort of, before the course."

"What happened?"

Then in a rush it all came up. "I think I'm a lesbian."

A slight smile crossed her face. "I'm not surprised."

"You're not?"

"Cath, it's plain as can be; when men talk you listen politely, but when women talk you listen with all your heart. Every woman that knows you is in love with you, loves being in your company."

I considered what she said. "So, do you love being in my company?"

"Of course, but I am not a lesbian."

"What if I am in love with you?"

"Cath, I love you but not the way you want, and need."

Nancy Phifer in her pink glasses, beautiful brown hair, and long limbs was, in that moment, one of the kindest women ever, one of the most helpful. I looked at her for a long time under the yellow light of the lamp above her table. She never looked away. It's easy to confuse tenderness with desire.

I thought that after my big sleep, I was slowly waking up. In reality, I was simply sitting with what I had said. As the time passed, I felt lighter. A part of me that I had been shutting away was finally settling in, finally arriving home. Forgiveness is an amazing thing; years later I would have the same feeling when I thoroughly cried over the accident and Rita's death, when I finally brought those feelings home instead of keeping them at bay.

"Have you told anyone else?" she asked.

"No. Who can I tell? No one will understand."

"Dail will understand."

Dail Bridges was another in that circle of friends I had made in Morganton, but she was also different. She was more than a friend; she was my best friend. Dail worked at the school for the deaf and had taught me enough sign language so that I could muddle my way through the challenges of an Outward Bound course with two of her brightest students: Scott and Dennis. These two young men on the verge of leaving the residential school that had held them so safely for all of their school-age years were leaving for college and the larger hearing world. They were also to be students in my Outward Bound crew. In the weeks and months that preceded their arrival on the course, Dail and I became very close. After the course, she and I had grown even closer as we helped Scott and Dennis prepare for college. Telling Nancy I was gay was one thing. Telling Dail meant risking rejection from someone who deeply mattered, whose friendship and respect felt utterly necessary. But I also thought that Nancy was right. If there was anyone who could hear and affirm that I was gay, it was Dail. So, a few weeks later I traveled to the camp where she worked in the shadow of Stone Mountain, a great granite dome rising out of the forested ridges and open valleys of the Southern Appalachians.

I arrived late into the evening; Dail had responsibilities to get her campers to bed, then we would be free to sit and talk. I remember the blanket of stars that covered our conversation that night, the warm air, and the smell of dry earth that surrounded us.

After a while of catching up, I broached the subject.

"I saw Phifer a few weeks ago."

"Nancy Phifer! How's she doin'?"

"She's good. She, we, talked and… Dail," I took a deep breath. "I think I'm a lesbian."

Silence. Then, "How do you know?"

"I don't know, I just know. I mean I have never had a serious boyfriend. I have never been attracted to men. I love being with women. I want… I want to make love with a woman." I finally said it, said what I had been thinking for so long ever since that night outside Becky's tent. I looked over at Dail but I couldn't read her face.

"Do you think it's wrong?"

"No. No, I don't. Cath Johnson, you are one of the most amazing women I know. If that's who you are, it doesn't change a thing with me."

Whatever else Dail said after that didn't matter. She was still my dear friend, and still is to this day. I never saw Nancy Phifer again, but I will be always grateful that her kindness helped me open the closet door.

During the following weeks, I began telling others that I was gay and each responded in much the same way: not surprised and glad that I had finally admitted it to myself. I began going to gay bars, playing women's rugby; I bought music by Chris Williamson, Holly Near, and Meg Christian, the champions of women's music in the day. It's funny how simple it all seemed after that; a woman on the staff who I had been spending increasing amounts of time with was clearly a love interest. All of my longings now made sense. The women I watched, wanted to spend time with, those I admired, were suddenly potential girlfriends. Women I might kiss, women I might—what? It seems unfathomable, 40 some years later, that I was so naïve. At 22, I still hadn't experienced the pleasures of sex: the deep kisses, the rush of hands, the urgent desire to touch, taste, and explore every curve and hollow of another's body. Eventually I would know all of this, but in the meantime I had more coming out to do.

That Christmas, my parents were spending a few weeks in Miami and I flew out from the Northwest to join them. Driving from the airport across Biscayne Bay in my father's convertible, I closed my eyes and let the sun and the salt air bathe my face. Even though it was only December, we in Olympia had endured more rain than most places get in a year.

Disembarking a plane in Phoenix once, I heard those who had come to meet Seattle friends exclaim, fondly, upon seeing them: "It's the moss people!" I admit that there have been winters here when I have looked in the mirror, sure that my skin had taken on a slightly greenish cast. It is always good to get away from the wet and into the sun.

Closing my eyes as we drove was also a way to avoid more than perfunctory conversation—something I had become adept at over the last few years. I kept to safe topics, stories of my recent adventures or future travel plans. Many visits I would arrive with a cold and promptly lose my voice. My mother worried that I worked too hard. That visit though, I had an agenda. I intended to come out first to my mother and then with her support and backing, to my father. I judged every moment, wondering if it was the one I should seize to speak.

Finally one night after finishing the dishes, my mother and I sat down to watch TV. My father had gone off to bed so it was just the two of us. She by then had drunk three martinis, a glass of wine, and now a shot of almond liqueur. Dressed in her silk pajamas and silk robe—I was still dressed from the beach in shorts and sweatshirt.

"Mom," I began, "I want to tell you something." I crossed to the television and turned down the sound.

"What, honey, is something wrong?" My mother shifted in her chair to face me in mine.

Although I had rehearsed for days a long preface that included important leading questions such as: "Haven't you ever wondered why I never had a serious boyfriend?" Or, "Haven't you ever wondered why I dress the way I do?" (Not exactly fashionable and certainly not very feminine.) Now that I had the moment, my heart raced; I could not remember my planned words except the essential sentence. "Mom, I'm gay."

Her face softened and then gave into some weight I could not see. "Is it anything that I did wrong?"

"No, Mom, you didn't do anything wrong."

My mother started to cry. "Please don't tell your father."

I felt so uncomfortable seeing her cry; hated being the cause of her pain. "Please don't cry."

"It's just that your life will be so hard."

"No it won't; it's already easier. Mom, please, don't worry."

"What about the church?"

"I don't go to church anymore." She raised her hand as if to push away what she had just heard. I think hearing that I no longer attended Mass was harder for her than hearing that I was gay. She lowered her hand and looked away, still crying. "Mom, it'll be alright. I'll be alright."

We sat in silence like that: she crying, me just waiting, feeling relieved to have spoken the truth to her and sad to see her pain. Finally she turned back to me.

"You won't tell your father."

"OK. I won't tell him."

"Promise?"

"I promise."

It seems stunning to me now, how often in my life I was willing to silence myself in order to protect others. It would be 15 years later, when I met the love of my life, that I finally came out to my father. I can't remember his initial response, but when I asked him if he was disappointed that I wasn't in love with a man, he shook his head then looked at me and said: "I probably wouldn't like the son of a bitch anyway." That was it, we never spoke of my gayness again. And while it took time, both my parents eventually accepted my sexual orientation and grew to truly support me. What a distance they traveled within the context of their Catholic faith, their Midwestern upbringings, and their mutual desire for harmony and order in the world that rarely obliges.

FERN CAVE

After 3 years of seasonal instructing, I was hired to work year-round in North Carolina. It was what I had dreamed of long ago as that shy 16-year-old student at the Minnesota School. Now I no longer returned to the Pacific Northwest after a summer of instructing but lived on the mountain, outside of Morganton, throughout the year. A core group of us minded the school through the winter months, performing much needed maintenance, teaching January winter courses, and otherwise staying in shape by climbing, paddling, and caving. The years I spent on the school's permanent staff were deeply rewarding. I became a course director, overseeing other instructors in the field. My own wilderness skills grew increasingly sophisticated and I discovered I had a natural ability for teaching. If once I had imagined a future as an Outward Bound instructor, I now imagined a future living and working at the North Carolina School for many years to come. But those ideas changed on a February caving trip in 1979.

A warm glow spilled from a small alcove where my friends waited. I couldn't see or hear them, but I knew they were there. For the first time that I could remember, I wished for companionship and security more than adventure. *I could just go back; let somebody else go first.* Sometimes it is simply better not to think, but focus on the task at hand. So, I checked my knots and the gates on my carabiners to be sure they were locked. I looked up, letting the beam from my headlamp find the anchor, two mud-caked steel bolts drilled into the cave's wall. Those bolts and a number of small details were about to hold my life. *Task at hand*, I thought, taking a deep breath. Then I switched off my headlamp, hauled up on the rappel rope, leaned back, and stepped into the void.

Fern Cave is located in northeastern Alabama where steep hill country rises above exhausted fields of tobacco and cotton. One of the deepest pit caves in the United States, Fern has a bell-shaped shaft that requires more than 400 feet of rope to descend. An accompanying underground waterfall presents an additional challenge to an already long descent. Four of us had come from the school to practice our vertical caving technique, the use of fixed ropes and mechanical devices to drop into, and climb out of, otherwise inaccessible portions of caves.

Stepping from solid footing at the edge of the pit, I dropped free for several feet and then swung into the force of the waterfall with a smack. Gallons of cold water poured over my head and down my back. Thankfully, it only took a few seconds for the rappel rope to pull me free. Now in line with the anchor above, I descended alongside the falling column of water into a surprising quiet. I hadn't known that water falls silently until it has something to fall over or against.

I fed the rappel rope slowly and carefully through the rack of aluminum bars controlling my descent. Rappelling too fast builds up heat and too much heat can melt a rope. Slowly I twirled in the quiet blackness, the exhilaration of the experience replacing my earlier anxiety.

For the last 7 years, I had made my life living out of a pack and the back of a pickup truck. I had spent whole seasons sleeping under tarps and in tents, had transient friendships and a few fleeting loves. The pastel streaks of dawn, the last whisper of wind, and first flicker of stars at dusk were all books that I had read many times, in the desert, on glaciers, and along the banks of Arctic rivers. I had gained a solid sense of myself, and enjoyed feeling competent, skilled, and strong. But that year I had begun to sense that my life was missing something. Something I did not know how to name but recognized when I drove through small towns on hot summer nights and saw whole families sitting on their porch steps laughing with neighbors. It was not something I actively thought about, but rather a fleeting feeling that came to me from time to time.

After 20 minutes, moving steadily down the rope, I began to hear the water again. It rose from below, first as a low rumble that grew steadily louder until it roared. When my feet finally touched down, a surge of wind, water, and sound made it almost impossible to stand upright. Struggling to keep my balance, I unclipped from the rope and gave it two hard tugs, signaling Doug, my caving partner, that the rope was free for him to come down.

It is typical caving protocol to rappel down alone and then climb out with a partner since the trip up is much more strenuous, takes twice the time, and is psychologically more challenging.

Now in the bottom of the pit, I looked for a place to get out of the wind and spray and wait. A large boulder at the edge of the shaft promised some protection. Once behind it, I relaxed: ate, drank some water, and got out of my harness. The minutes passed slowly. Even with the food and relative shelter, a damp cold spread through me. Shivering, I wondered about the other pair of cavers, middle-aged men from Tennessee, who had rappelled down in front of me.

Hypothermia is a genuine concern in a wet cave, and up top I had questioned the two whether their blue jeans and sweatshirts would keep them warm enough. Beneath our caving coveralls we wore polypropylene long underwear, wool sweaters, and kayak paddling jackets.

"Aren't you worried about getting cold?" I had asked.

Bob, the older and more experienced of the two, replied, "Nah, if y'all keep movin', you'll stay warm." His slow Smoky Mountain drawl sounded confident, if not slightly patronizing.

"What about the waterfall?" I continued.

Al, who had never made a long drop, chimed in with an overly loud voice, "It's just a little shower." Then with a hint of nervousness, "Ain't that right, Bob?"

I had looked to my partner Doug for some support, but he busily chipped mud from the soles of his boots and said nothing. At the time, I thought he was just uninterested. Looking back, I wonder if his silence wasn't a way of saving face for Bob and Al, demonstrating his loyalty to the culture of men.

Every few minutes I peered over the top of the boulder to see if I could spot Doug coming down. Each time, I was assaulted by a blast of wind and spray. Finally, a tiny dot of light blinked on, then off. As Doug neared the bottom, it blinked on and stayed on. Like landing lights, I thought as I went to greet him.

"Wow!" Doug yelled. "What a ride! Can you believe this water?" He tugged hard on the rope, twice. Doug's image was a blur because of the spray in my face, yet I could see that something was very wrong. He pointed over my shoulder. Al was headed our way from the back of the pit, supporting a stumbling Bob. Doug immediately grabbed the rappel rope and tugged hard, three times—signaling trouble. He waited a moment and then did it again. Our other two friends would now wait up above, anxiously wondering.

We hurried to the stumbling Tennessee cavers. Doug grabbed Bob's other arm, and together with Al, dragged him over to the boulder. Bob was barely conscious. His face looked ashen, his skin was cold, and his pulse weak.

"Hypothermia?" Doug yelled, both asking a question and stating the obvious. "We got to get him up."

"He can't climb like this. He's too out of it," I said, shoving a bag of trail mix at Al, whose hands shook so badly that he spilled the first handful before he got it to his mouth. Doug stripped off Bob's sweatshirt and T-shirt. They were completely soaked. He took the garbage bag from inside his helmet liner, poked a hole in the bottom of it with his fist, and pulled it over Bob's head like a poncho. Neither of us recalled saying anything to the other, or ever having been taught what to do next. But somehow we knew. I took the carbide lamp from my pack, filled it, and lit it. We carried the dependable miners' lamps as a back-up source of light. The little flame burned yellow for a second, then hot blue-white. Doug held the plastic bag out and away from Bob's chest; I moved my lamp under it, being careful not to burn Bob or melt the bag. Doug instructed Al to remove his wet clothes, then use the garbage bag from my helmet and his carbide lamp to create a heat tent for himself. Al warmed up quickly; it took Bob longer: 15 minutes before he could answer questions coherently, 30 minutes before he was fully aware of his surroundings.

When I considered the seriousness of our situation, my chest would go tight, so I kept my attention focused on Bob. When he could finally hold the lamp for himself, it was time to go.

Doug was the obvious choice to go up with Bob. He was much stronger than me and could help Bob more easily if needed. As Bob started up the rope, I could see that each step would be an effort. If he lost consciousness on the way up, it would be a nightmare for Doug, for us all.

"Hurry up—OK?" I yelled, giving Doug a quick hug while the water beat against us. "I don't want to stay down here forever." I hoped that I sounded optimistic. In truth, I was scared.

"Take care," Doug yelled, as the waterfall's wind blew his words away.

Our caving harnesses, with ascending devices sewn in, attached us to the rope in three places: the left shoulder, right knee, and left foot. Ascending devices when un-weighted move along a fixed rope easily, once weighted they lock into place. The design of our harnesses enabled us to climb the rope like stairs: step-by-step without the need for hands or upper arm strength. By being attached at the shoulder, we remained upright and close to the rope while our legs did the work.

Doug and Bob quickly disappeared into the darkness while I hurried back to the rock where Al was waiting. Al and I took turns sharing the lamp. The first time I placed it beneath my paddling jacket and felt the heat spread out across my chest, I felt sleepy. Realizing how chilled I had become, I ate more food, drank more water, and concentrated on what was to happen next. The minutes dragged by. When I would look up at the tiny bits of light, I was grateful to see that Doug and Bob were making progress, but I wished they would move faster. Al and I made a few attempts at conversation but the effort required too much energy. So we lapsed into silence, each of us lost in our thoughts.

At the time I was in my mid-twenties. Why, I wondered, was I taking trips that seemed to be getting riskier? More and more, I felt uneasy in demanding situations. *You are losing your confidence,* a voice within me chided. While there was truth in the statement, there was also a part of me who saw that my priorities were changing, and who knew it was time to rethink my life.

When 45 minutes had passed, I went over to the rope. It was still weighted. Twice more I would check, twice more I would return to the rock behind which Al and I hid. Finally on the third time, after 1 hour and 10 minutes, the rope was free. Bob and Doug were up. A wave of relief ran through me and filled me with determination.

Al clipped in and started up. I followed quickly behind him. The storm of water and wind raged, but an even larger fury was driving me. I wanted out of this pit, and out of this cave. Climbing fast, I hoped that I would get warmer as we went, but instead got colder. Whenever I stopped to catch my breath, my teeth would chatter so hard my jaw ached, and all my joints felt brittle.

First, Al would climb. When he stopped to rest, I would climb up until I was directly underneath him. Then, while I rested, he would start again. We climbed like that: up, out of the water, and into the quiet. The silence that had been peaceful on the way down was nerve racking on the way up. I strained to hear the slightest rumble of water above. When I could hear it, the top would be getting close.

Al was right above me and not moving. "You OK?" I asked. "Al, are you OK?" I spoke louder. "Al?" There was a rising edge in my voice. "Al, talk to me!" I reached up, grabbed his pants leg, and shook it.

"Unh?"

His voice sounded flat and vacant. There was a long pause and then, "I'm OK."

"Are you sure?" I didn't wait for an answer. "Listen," I said, speaking fast. "I'll call it out. OK? We'll go ten steps and stop. OK? Here we go. One!" I was relieved when he raised his right leg and stepped up. "Two!" He raised his left leg. "Three!" He made the ten steps and I followed up beneath him as fast as I could. I forgot that I was cold; I forgot about listening for the water; I forgot everything, except how to count to ten. When I swallowed, I found my stomach in my throat. Every now and then I tried to talk to Al, but he did not answer. The fact that he kept climbing was enough. I don't know how many times I counted to ten. We kept making progress and that was all I dared think about. Finally, I heard a low sound traveling down the rope.

"Al, listen. Hear it? The waterfall, we're gonna make it!" I started to offer non-stop encouragement while still counting out steps. Sound filled the space. It grew in decibels as we went. Spray made it hard to see, but I screamed out the count, hoping Al would keep following it.

When my helmet bumped into Al's foot, I panicked. "Al!" I screamed. There was no response. I wedged my body up the rope until my shoulder was under his butt. "Come on, Al," I said through my teeth as I lifted my right leg as high as I could, grabbed the rope with both hands, and stood up. Al moved up the rope. I raised my left leg and pushed, moving him up a few more feet. He was dead weight. I knew this could be done, but I was not sure I had the strength to do it. I raised my head, looking for the top of the pit and got a faceful of water. In that moment I hated everything. I hated being stuck in a cave, on a rope, at the edge of a waterfall, with a man too stupid to dress for the conditions. Using this anger, I pushed Al up a few more steps. Then he moved on his own. "Alright," I said. It was as much a prayer of thanks as anything. "Go, Al. Go!"

Climbing one step at a time, I could now see lights above us. Suddenly we were being hauled up through the waterfall. Al disappeared. I took a step and felt hands grab ahold of my harness and drag me up over the edge of the shaft. It was Mike, one of our group. When he hugged me to him, I held on hard.

After warming up again with carbide lamps and hot drinks, we headed out. Mike had fixed safety lines in the stream passage. Due to heavy rains on the surface, the water in the stream had been rising all afternoon. What had been knee-deep coming in, was now up to our chests on the way out. Without the ropes, we wouldn't have been able to pull ourselves against the current. Finally, we left the stream passage. I got a whiff of fresh air—sweet and warm. I wanted to run to that smell. I was not the only one. All of us scrambled quickly over boulders, hurrying towards the entrance. Finally a small patch of pale light appeared in the distance. I felt like crying.

When we reached the entrance of the cave, it was evening. But after the solid darkness of the earth, the blue-black sky seemed luminous. Dry clothes we had stashed going in felt incredibly good; running shoes, like moccasins on my feet. As we hiked down through the forest, a sliver of moon rose over flooded fields below. By the time we reached the road, we were full of laughter, congratulating ourselves on our skill and our good luck. Bob and Al even joined in, although they were understandably subdued. Back at our cars, they thanked each of us. In their eyes was a depth and sincerity that had not been there before. We shook hands all around and watched them go, a pair of red taillights heading for the highway. After a hot meal and more recounting of the day's events, we four threw our sleeping bags out beside the road.

Even though I was deeply tired and the frogs had quieted and Orion was rising overhead, I could not sleep. The sense that I had come to the end of something filled me with a small and grateful sadness. In the sounds of that country night, I could hear a purpose larger than my own calling softly to me. I could not have explained it then, I only knew the feel of its tug on my heart.

Not long after the caving trip, I learned that Willi Unsoeld had been killed in an avalanche on Mount Rainier in Washington. A young student had also died with him. The day I heard the news, I hiked up the tallest mountain near our Outward Bound base camp to be alone and watch the sun set from its rocky summit. At first my steps had been heavy and slow. Then, they became furious and fast. I broke into a run and when I reached the summit, my heart was pounding and I gasped for breath. When I sat down, chest heaving, I started to cry. It seemed I hadn't cried in years. Maybe I hadn't.

"How do you handle death?" I remembered Willi's question and his response. "You don't handle death. Death handles you." My tears continued to stream down my face while the sky burned a fiery Appalachian orange. Soon bands of soft purple and velvet pink appeared. A thousand feet below me, Linville Gorge darkened into night. An evening breeze came up. My first teacher of risk and death was gone, the man who challenged my doubts and encouraged my Outward Bound dreams—gone. But Willi never reserved a place for sentimentality. He would want us all to go on teaching others about the wilderness and themselves. "C'mon, Johnson," I said aloud, in the way he would have said it. I headed back down the trail as the first stars shone overhead.

Willi was fond of saying, "It doesn't matter what it is, you have to have something to fight. Doesn't have to be a mountain, but it has to be something. And it isn't important whether you win or lose. Only that you keep fighting."

Even though I felt called towards a future I couldn't see, I knew that leaving North Carolina and returning to Washington seemed like the first step. The decision would be another watershed moment in my life: separating who I had been from who I would become.

CARMELITES

There's a family story that my mother loved to tell, one that I never tired of hearing. It reflected the innocence of another time and the way in which I have, since birth, been at home in the company of women.

When I was just a few days old, not much more than a hungry mouth, the smallest of hands, and softest of skin, with a few strands of light brown hair pasted on my head and a pair of shiny black eyes, my mother and father introduced me to the Sisters of Carmel. These women, educated and bright, had given their lives to God through cloistered meditation, silence, and prayer. "They were your very first friends," my mother would say as she recalled the story.

We were on our way home from the hospital. Your father was driving his new red Pontiac convertible with its white top. It was a beautiful May afternoon. On any other day he would have put the top down, you know Dad, but that day he thought it might be too cold for his new baby girl. We had you in the back seat in our laundry basket. They didn't have car seats back then like they do now.

I can imagine the scene: my mother, wearing a now looser-fitting, mint green maternity dress, her short brown hair freshly washed and neatly bobbed. I can see her sitting close to my father on the Pontiac's big leather bench seat, leisurely smoking a cigarette. Having given them up for her entire pregnancy, it was the first thing she asked for when she awoke from anesthesia and found that she had delivered a healthy baby girl. As they drive, she savors each deep inhalation. My father, in his starched white shirt and bright blue tie, drives with one hand on the wheel, the other draped across my mother's shoulders. He is a little stunned by what has happened and every so often looks in the rearview mirror just to be sure it is true. In the back seat sits a wicker laundry basket: the same one that he and my mother have carried a hundred times up and down the three flights of stairs that separate their apartment from the laundry room in their apartment's basement. Now instead of dirty clothes, that basket is lined with cotton bedding in which his new daughter sleeps. He feels proud and decides we should stop at the Carmelite Monastery before heading home.

Carmel of the Resurrection Monastery was situated in a park-like setting dotted with hardwood trees, on the west side of Indianapolis. The Monastery looked as if it had been lifted out of the Middle Ages with gray stone turrets and arched walkways, wrought iron railings and heavy grates. Later in life while traveling in southern France, I saw many similar structures, abbeys built in the 14th century. The Carmel I knew, however, had been built in the 1920s and set down, not in the south of France, but in a Midwestern city famous for its trade in hogs and corn, and for its motor speedway. As a child growing up, Carmel was as much a part of my life as the Indy 500.

When we arrived at the Monastery, Dad carried you up the steps and through the big wooden doors. Once inside it took a few moments for our eyes to adjust. It had been so bright outside and you know how dim it is in there. When we could finally see, we went into the turn room and pulled the chain that rang the bell on the other side.

It only took a minute until someone arrived and we heard the small wooden door slide back.

"Hello? Is someone there?"

You know how clear and youthful the sisters' voices sound, hidden behind the grate. They sound like angels.

The "turn room" was named for a 3-foot-high revolving wooden door that served as an interface between the cloister and the outside world. Beside the wooden turn was a little window cut through the stone, with an iron grate across it and a black curtain on the other side that maintained the integrity of the cloister. The turn room was the room where short visits and small business occurred.

"Bill and Cay Johnson, Sister," your father announced as always.

He had been visiting the Carmelites for many years; Karlyboy and Rosie used to take him when he was a boy.

"Oh, Bill and Cay," the voice spoke with obvious gladness. "This is Sister Rachel, how are you both?"

"Just fine Sister, we brought our Cathy for a visit."

Sister Rachel gasped, a small rush of breath, and then a joyful exhale. "Cathy."

She said your name as if you were someone long awaited.

The sisters, although cloistered, were fully aware of the events of the world both large and small and they followed the lives of their friends with close attention.

"She's so beautiful. You won't believe her."

In this part of the story, my mother would grow misty-eyed. For years I didn't understand her tenderness. Not until I had children in my own life did I comprehend how challenging it is to release them into the care of others, into the world. I was only 4 days old and my mother was about to give me from her arms.

Then, your father rolled open the turn. It always smelled musty and a little sweet—from the fresh bread, I think.

The sisters of Carmel were known for their cinnamon raisin bread. It was a small cottage industry that brought revenue into their community.

He placed you, in your laundry basket, inside the turn, then slowly passed the wood against the palms of his hands, giving you 'round to the other side.

On several occasions I have dreamed of lyrical voices, laughing and cooing, of a profound sense of being cherished and held. When I have awoken, I know this is my dream of that first visit. After passing me to the sisters, my parents stepped outside for another cigarette.

We could hear the sisters giggling, laughing, and cooing with you even outside. They loved meeting you.

"Thank you for sharing her with us, Cay." Sister Miriam, the new Reverend Mother, spoke from behind the shrouded grate as I took you back into my arms. *"She is truly beautiful."*

"Oh, I know that, Mother."

"Sister Anne will love to meet little Cathy. I'm sorry she isn't here, Bill. You must promise to go out and visit her—soon."

"We will have to do that."

Sister Anne Clem had been one of the founding sisters of the Carmel community at Indianapolis, and over the years of visiting the monastery as a young man, my father had grown very fond of her. When I was born he insisted my middle name be hers—Ann. And although she had left Indianapolis the year before I was born, he took great joy in introducing me to her community. As I was growing up he often referred to Sr. Anne, reminding me that I was named for her. "Maybe someday we'll go visit her at the monastery in Reno," he would say, but we never did.

"The Carmelites were truly your very first friends," Mom would re-iterate as she finished the story. Then she would give me a hug. "You must always stay close to them."

One of the ways I coped with the accident and Rita's death was by running. I ran by leaving Indiana, by keeping busy and challenged, by proving to myself over and over that I was capable, trustworthy, and responsible. Yet, no matter how many times I proved this, it was never enough. I was never satisfied. I felt driven by a discontent that I did not understand, always searching for someplace where, or someone with whom, I could rest. I didn't comprehend then that the work was within and I could never be satisfied by achievements, by friends, or by lovers. I kept forcing everything that happened behind me, yet it always stayed strangely in front, like a horizon I could not escape and was always driving towards.

A year after I left North Carolina, I took a climbing trip in the desert Southwest and found myself driving through Reno, Nevada. I would like to pretend that I was unaware of Reno's significance and that my arrival there was merely a coincidence. It was not. My decision to pass through Reno was based in my desire to feel something familiar, something comforting, to find welcome in a world that never quite felt like home. I was tired of running, but had no idea how to stop.

The Carmelite Monastery at Reno was nothing like the one I knew in Indianapolis. Situated on a suburban hillside, it looked more like a private residence than a Catholic cloister. I had been climbing in Joshua Tree National Park for a month and happened to be passing through Nevada when I hit upon the idea of finding Sr. Anne. The address had been easy to locate. I simply looked it up in the phone book while getting gas. It was late afternoon and I was tired of driving. Why not, I thought, and rang the bell.

A short elderly woman with beautiful white hair, cut stylishly short, answered the door. She was wearing a blue skirt and white blouse. Had she also not been wearing a carved wooden cross, I might have second-guessed the address. I hadn't realized how much I associated the cool darkness of the turn room, the mysterious feminine voices speaking from the other side of a curtained grate, with my experience of the Carmelites. Now face-to-face with a very ordinary-looking older woman, I felt a little disoriented and self-conscious about my appearance.

Worn jeans, a bright blue tank top, and flip-flops: these were hardly the clothes I would have chosen had I really been thinking about what I was doing and who I was about to meet.

"I'm looking for the Carmelite Monastery."

"You have found us. May I help you?" There was a hint of southern drawl in the older woman's voice, the way she said the word *help*.

"My name is Cathy Johnson. I am looking for Sister Anne."

"Cathy Johnson?" The woman looked at me with an open curiosity and a brightness I usually associate with children. "I am Sister Anne. Do I know you?"

I started to feel uneasy, not at all sure why I had come, let alone for what was I looking. What did I want from this elderly woman? I had given no real thought to any of it.

"I think you know me, I'm Bill Johnson's daughter, from Indianapolis; my middle name is Ann."

The older woman standing in front of me raised her hand to her mouth, her eyes widened, and then she smiled sweetly. "Oh my word. Come in, Ann."

For our entire conversation and in the few letters we exchanged in the years following, she always addressed me as Ann. To her, I was truly a namesake. She was interested in and seemed knowledgeable about my work with Outward Bound.

"Young people need strong experiences," she said.

She also had many questions about my folks and grandmother Rosie, about their health, their happiness. She hadn't known that my grandmother had died that previous fall.

"Your grandparents were so very good to us. When we desperately needed a new roof, your grandfather came through with the money. It was a large sum in those days."

I knew Karlyboy and Rosie had been very devoted to the church and it did not surprise me that they had paid for the monastery's new roof. It was easy to fill in the blanks, recent history, and current facts for Sr. Anne; her questions were simple. The ones I carried were more complicated. Swimming just below the surface of my awareness, I wanted to know: do our lives have a purpose, do the events of our lives serve that purpose, can God be disappointed in us? Ultimately, I wondered if God was disappointed in me. In my dreams, I believed this woman might have those answers, but I couldn't find the courage to ask.

Our time together passed quickly; a bell rang for divine office, the prayers before supper. She asked if I wanted to join the community for prayers and the evening meal. I was too shy, by then telling myself that I had taken up too much of her time. Today, I would gladly accept that invitation, grateful for the time in quietude, reflection, and prayer. But in those days it would have been too risky to enter into such quiet. All the feelings I kept buried by being on the move, seeking adventures, and staying busy might catch up with me. This was not a considered thought, but simply the way I lived. I declined her invitation. She gave me a hug and made me promise to remember her to my parents.

There are still times when I feel alone, confused, and lost—not sure that I am worthy of love or have a place where I belong. When these times visit, I think of that community of women who first held and loved me like one of their own. I imagine that I have a place there among them, in the silence and the solitude.

HEARING LOSS

Returning to the Northwest, to Olympia, Washington, I finally finished my undergraduate degree at the place it had begun 10 years earlier—at Evergreen. Six months later, in the spring of 1983, I got a job at my new alma mater managing the college swimming pool and teaching outdoor recreation classes. I was 28 years old. I moved into a small rental house, planted some flowers, and got a cat. Just like that, I felt quite settled but also lonely, and I began to notice that I was having trouble hearing.

My hearing left slowly, the way one season changes to another, with little hints along the way—the first cool nights, a dab of color in the trees. It was a similar process for my hearing. When others spoke, I began noticing how often I said, "Huh?" I became aware of those who stopped to listen, while I kept on talking, who went to pick up phones that never rang for me, whose words piled up in a jumble at the end of their sentences—leaving me to pick out the meaning from a hundred possibilities, which made for some humorous misinterpretations. "Let's go back to the house and have sex," was in truth only an invitation for "snacks." A request for a box, I answered by bringing a pair of socks. Not all the mistakes were funny. There were a growing number of frustrating misunderstandings as well. Cashiers waited impatiently for more change when fifty cents became confused with fifteen. A routine traffic stop went awry when I started explaining where I was heading when the officer had asked if I knew how fast I was going. Initially, when friends suggested that I get my hearing tested I put them off, saying I didn't think it was that bad. A few mistakes, a little embarrassment, none of it seemed to warrant that much concern. Then one day, out running, I grasped that I really was losing my hearing.

It was a cold morning, early in March, but the sun warmed my face as I ran around Capitol Lake, so named for Washington's Capitol in Olympia. The lake lies just below the capitol campus. Running the lake was a favorite route of mine. Well lit, the right distance, and wild enough to distract me from the busy, urban environment. Birdlife was abundant near the lake, and through the comings and goings of different species, I could track the seasons changing.

That particular morning as I ran, I noticed that the marsh along the lake's edge had filled with red-winged blackbirds, unmistakable in their shiny black feathers and bright red and yellow epaulets. *These are the first I've seen this year* I marveled, thinking that spring was surely on the way. A hundred or more crowded the brown cattails and green sedges. *But where was their call?* The question stopped me immediately. Still breathing heavily, I stood and listened. I could hear the traffic passing. I could hear industrial sounds from the seaport behind me where cranes and forklifts loaded and unloaded container ships, but no birds. I approached the water's edge. Several birds flushed, but plenty remained unperturbed. I crossed my arms tightly over my chest to keep warm as I scanned the marshy area before me. Quickly, I found what I was looking for—a bird singing: a plump male perched on a fuzzy brown cattail with his head tilted back, opening and closing his beak in song. I don't know how long I watched that bird and then others, each opening his mouth, making a territorial declaration, announcing the arrival of a mate, or soliciting for one, but I heard none of it.

I walked home putting the evidence together and before I finished breakfast, I had an appointment with an audiologist to have my hearing tested.

The audiologist, a petite woman about my age with blonde hair worn tightly pulled back and large glasses that hid her face behind an air of intellectual importance, ushered me into a soundproof booth.

"Go ahead and sit down."

No small talk here, just business, I thought as I sat down in a comfortable chair that swiveled easily on its pedestal. It took some willpower to resist the temptation to turn back and forth as the audiologist placed a set of headphones over my ears. Even though I knew that I was having difficulty hearing, I really did not expect to find out anything unusual. I fully expected to be tested and sent upon my way, a *take two aspirins and call me in the morning* approach.

With the heavy headphones rubber cupping my ears, I looked about the booth. The lighting was dim and the walls including the door were lined with white acoustic tiles. Were it not for the window in front of me, the space would have been disturbingly small, and now that the door was closed, airless.

Airless, I thought. *That's what has happened to my relationship.* Over the last year, my relationship with a lover had deflated into a flat and stale existence. We were both a little lost. When she had taken a mountain guiding job in Europe, I hated her for leaving. She had gone with no end date and no return ticket.

"I need to go," she had said, "for my own sanity."

After 3 or 4 months, a few letters, and one or two phone calls, I had an affair with someone else: a not-so-brave way of letting her know just how angry I felt. She was shocked. I didn't care. When she finally did come back, I was gone. Now sitting in the sound booth, I felt tired thinking about it. Whatever playful mood I had been in a few minutes ago had been replaced by one sour and sad.

The audiologist took her seat on the other side of the window, then placed her hands lightly on a console of switches and dials. I watched as her fingers danced over them with the dexterity of a musician. Then, her voice came booming out of nowhere.

"How's this volume?"

"A little loud."

"Is this better?"

I nodded then realized she was waiting for a reply. "Yes, it's better."

"I will be giving you a series of tones. First, in your right ear; just raise your right hand when you hear the tone."

Small hands moved slowly over the dials. There was no sound, only a faint fuzzy noise, one that I always heard when things were quiet. The audiologist looked up at me, our eyes met, then she moved the dial some more. A sound, like a faraway channel marker in the fog, came through. I raised my right hand. The distant foghorn was followed by the flip of another switch, by a look, a turning of another dial, the presence of a new sound—this time a little hum. It went on for a while: low tones, high tones, and mid tones interspersed with each other. Then we switched to the left ear. After that, I received a different kind of headphone, one that conducts sound through the temporal bones: first on the right side, then on the left. The test ended with me sitting in the booth looking through the window at the audiologist, repeating a series of words that she spoke.

"Say *bat boy.*"

"Bad boy."

"Say *baseball.*"

"Baseball."

"Say *fairway.*"

"Stairway."

Finally the test was over. She made notations on a clipboard, got up from her chair, and opened the door to the booth with a whoosh. When she removed the headphones, I stood up.

"Your change," she said, pointing to a handful of change that had fallen from my pocket to the floor.

In her office, the audiologist reviewed my audiogram with me. "You have a mild to moderate sensori-neural hearing loss."

"What does that mean?"

"It means that the loss occurs due to inner ear or nerve impairment. I recommend a hearing aid for your right ear. You may eventually need one for your left as well. You should be reevaluated on an annual basis to monitor the nature of the loss."

I had not imagined this outcome, but the audiologist seemed matter of fact about it. For my part, I did not question the diagnosis or the prescription. I took the information and ordered the hearing aid she suggested, not unlike the way someone would order a pair of glasses or agree to orthodontics. A few years later, when I was forced to order another for my other ear, I felt a little fearful. Maybe I would lose my hearing altogether. When I feel fearful, I usually take practical action. As a result, I began re-learning sign language, made friends in the local deaf community, bought an assistive listening device for my phone, and started moving through the world as a person with a disability.

Living with a hearing loss was challenging, but it also taught me compassion and opened me to grace.

ROWING

Deep in my psyche I believed that I was unloveable because of Rita's death; I believed I could never again be that good little girl whom God loved. I could not explain this at the time; I only knew that I felt a continuous need to push myself, to prove to myself that I was responsible, to challenge myself to be "good." Initially, I accomplished this by leading others in the wilderness. Now in my thirties, living and working back in Olympia, I turned to rowing to meet that need. I bought a single scull and fell in love with the boat and the sport.

My scull was long in the same way that I am tall. Sleek and fast, her hull was the color of sunset, her decking the color of unclouded sky. Each morning before lifting her from the racks, I would stop and admire her, touch her fondly, allow my hand to slide the length of her delicate cedar skin. With not-so-shy fingers, I traced the dark grains in her wood—and like a reader of palms, imagined that I could cipher her life from those lines. At 26 feet long, 14 inches wide at the beam, she tapered to less than an inch at either end. My single racing scull weighed just under 30 pounds fully rigged and was built specifically for me: my weight, my height, my reach. That boat was the epitome of craftsmanship, elegance, and speed. For 5 years, she carried my dreams and me over the waters of my life.

It was a Sunday morning, in June of 1987—the sky was growing lighter by the minute and the running clock mounted between my feet displayed the time elapsed: 4 minutes, 57 seconds. *Build it now*, I picked up the pace, *only a minute left.* Driving my legs down, I started counting out the strokes: "One, two, three," *faster, c'mon.* "Eight, nine, ten," *that's it.* The boat shot through the water towards the dock that served as my finish line. Meanwhile a firestorm raged through my body: thighs burst into flames, back muscles sparked and exploded, ribs separated and the tendons in my forearms stretched to the breaking. In the final seconds of a rowing race, even one that is simply against the clock, blood screams through the arteries and heart valves open and close with audible force, or at least that is how it seems. The world slips out of focus and the mind with its thousand doors closes down, so that only the one door—counting out the strokes—remains. Reach, catch, drive with the legs… the same set of motions repeat, until a clock or a finish line grants rest. *Drive it home. That's it. Last stroke, and—glide...* Lowering my hands, the boat sailed noiselessly past the dock.

To anyone watching from the shore I was simply a rower, out in the harbor early on a summer morning, not much more than a dark silhouette against a peach-colored sky. However, to those who lived along this protected Puget Sound inlet, I had become a customary sight. For 4 years I had trained here daily, racing back and forth before the grand houses with their large decks, and the old cabins tucked behind crumbling bulkheads. Even though I had not met the inhabitants of these structures, I considered them my neighbors; I would like to believe they thought similarly of me. Even in winter, when the early morning water and sky were poured like ink, their familiar shapes in yellow windows were a comfort. If rowing is the ultimate team sport, single sculling is its loneliest endeavor.

Lowering my oars onto the water, I gulped in mouthfuls of air. I had crossed the finish line in just under 6 minutes, a personal best. After months, really years of training, I was ready, ready for the National Championships. A satisfied smile spread across my sweating face and I felt like laughing out loud.

At the end of the week, I would load my scull onto a trailer headed for Indianapolis, Indiana, site of the United States Rowing Championships. Everything that I had worked for over the last 5 years was about to be rewarded. All the cold wet miserable mornings, all the tortuous workouts that taught me to push my body beyond its pain, all the doubt that constantly threatened the discipline, and all the times I said "No" to dinners, parties, events, and gatherings in order to be in bed before 9:00 PM were now worth it. Not only was I going to Indianapolis, I had a chance for a medal there, maybe even an invitation to a U.S. Olympic Team Development Camp. What had begun 5 years ago as a small desire—to learn how to scull, had grown into a bold and all-consuming dream—to be a National Champion.

I sculled my boat a bit, practiced a few drills, and considered whether or not to row one more race piece. My heart and respiration rates had returned to normal and I was thrilled by how well and how fast I was moving the boat. The temptation to train harder always increases as a competition nears, the very time when the body needs to restore itself. I considered this as the sun rose over the Cascades, spilling the day's new light onto the water.

Fourteen years had passed since the car accident and Rita's death. For most of those years, I had wandered through my life, accepting whatever opportunity fate presented. To family and friends, I appeared confident and sure. I went on wilderness trips, found engaging work, accumulated enough college credits for a degree, and had my first real relationships. But inside I still felt lost, and restless, never satisfied. I was aware that I was still searching for something, but I could not explain what. Forgiveness, redemption, love, home? Each sounded like a worthy aspiration, but never turned out to be the grail. If you don't know what it is you're searching for, you can't ask directions. And every day I wondered if I had already walked right by it, or missed it like an exit on the freeway a hundred miles back. In high school I had been someone who looked into the distance, picked a point, and walked to it. After the accident I became someone who simply followed whatever trail she was on until it met another, and then without looking either forward or back, would follow that path until it too branched.

Rowing had focused my attention and being on the water gave me a sense of peace that was otherwise tough to find. Rowing also gave me an identity, a persona that others admired, including me.

As with most dreams, the daily work of manifesting them is hard, sometimes pure drudgery. When I first bought my boat, I rented a moldy two-bedroom house trailer on a small lake outside of town, bought a set of weights, and set about mastering the art of sculling.

That first year I struggled to learn how to scull. The boat was never set. Instead, it tipped frustratingly from side to side. I stayed cautiously close to shore, plucking at the water with my oars. Most days, I paddled more than I rowed. The knuckles on my right hand became permanently nicked and scabbed from the fingernails on my left hand, which raked over them on every stroke. Still, I kept my daily appointment with the water and the boat. Gradually, I got better. Summer moved across the hills, leaving yellow alders and red maples in its wake. A pair of loons took up residence in the rushes not far from my dock and a flock of geese stopped over on their way to somewhere else. Throughout the fall I continued to flail about, row in circles, and otherwise battle for balance. There must have been a hundred times that I swore I would quit, but then made just enough progress to try again the next day. Finally, in winter, when a paper-thin layer of ice had just started spreading from the shore, I got it.

It was a January afternoon; the sky was overcast, looking like it could rain or snow at any minute. By the time I rowed to the end of the lake, the day's light was going. Having warmed up, I removed my sweater and my hat, and stuffed them down into the small space at my feet. I started back, dressed only in light fleece tights and shirt. On the third or fourth stroke something jerked my port oar; I had caught it on a submerged buoy line. Like a huge python, the dark water opened and swallowed, first the oar, then oarlock. It made its way slowly up the rigger and then pulled the boat over with it. There was nothing I could do except give myself to the lake.

The water was freezing; I gasped loudly as I surfaced. Treading water, I up-righted the boat and looked anxiously around. In the dim light I could see that there was no one on the shore, no lights in any of the trailers or cabins. There was no one to help me. In those days of thin wooden boats, it was easy to break them climbing back in, and while I knew theoretically how to re-enter my boat, I had never tried. Afraid to hurt my delicate boat, I decided to swim her into shore.

It didn't take long; the cold seeped into my body, making my legs heavy and weak. I was in serious trouble. Stopping and once again treading water, I got the oars into the right position and held them with one hand; with the other, I grabbed hold of the handle behind my seat. I took a deep breath, gave one hard kick, and pulled myself into the boat. As I did, I heard a loud crack. I kept going anyway. Once I got re-situated, I started to row. My teeth clattered and I could barely feel my hands. I needed to get warm; I needed to get home. Without thinking, I rowed harder and faster. A minute or two passed before I warmed up enough to realize what I was doing. I was sculling—not perfectly, but well. I applied more pressure with my legs, feeling each stroke grow longer and more powerful. I moved my hands faster, and drove my legs even harder. Then I felt, for the first time that year, what every rower loves to feel—the boat running out beneath her. The dangerousness of my situation in the water had burned through my tentativeness and I rowed with a new confidence and gritty determination.

That was 5 years earlier; now on a glorious June morning, I was sitting in that same boat. The long crack in its coxcomb from my cold water re-entry was still visible and the repair job still holding. Nationals were a little more than a week away. Five years of rowing had given me purpose, passion, and daily direction. I felt deeply satisfied. I took a sip from my water bottle and started rowing to the dock when something caught my attention.

Over on the shore a woman was moving across her deck. She was watering a series of hanging pots, each heavy with red and purple fuchsias. As she passed from one to the next, the water spilled over the tops and down the sides. Soon a line of little showers was falling in the morning light, watery curtains of shimmering diamonds in the distance. The sound of it traveled over the still air and I thought I heard her humming. It was beautiful, and sad.

Why sad? I wondered, surprised by my reaction. I couldn't answer my question because my throat started to tighten and my chest felt like someone was standing on it. The thought that maybe I was suffering a heart attack ran through my mind. As it did, my eyes filled with tears. I kept trying to regain my composure but the more I struggled for control, the harder I cried. Sitting in my thin and fragile boat, perched just inches above the water, I sobbed. Trying to hang on to what felt like sanity, I gripped the oars tighter. I gripped them so tight that my hands shook and the boat started tipping. Had the woman on the shore looked, she would have seen nothing unusual, no cause for alarm, just a rower resting a few yards off her beach. Meanwhile, I shook like someone beginning a seizure, my vision blurred, and I was unable to get my breath.

I didn't cry easily. My tears embarrassed me. I had invested a great deal in appearing strong and thought that crying was a sign of weakness. But as I watched that woman water her flowers, my heart started breaking. That thing for which I had been looking was right in front of my eyes. I could sense it, but not see it. I knew its presence, but not its name. Perhaps that is what caused me to panic: having found the object of my search and still not be able to name it, I felt utterly hopeless. Looking back at that morning, I now understand what was happening. Rowing had slowly taught me to love myself, to appreciate my beauty and my grace, my strength and my perseverance. Rowing had opened my heart.

In looking so hard for "home," the feeling that I belonged someplace in the world, I had become a wanderer. What I was looking for was rest from the searching. I needed to welcome home that part of me who felt as if she would never belong. I was convinced that I was unworthy and unwanted. In truth I had been well-loved by my family, my friends, and lovers, but so little of their affection ever found me. I had made myself unreachable, searching for something I would never find outside of my own heart. For years I had hated myself, beat myself, and rejected myself; in doing so, I had often pushed others away.

A sharp pain stopped the panic and made me sit up, wide-eyed and alert. Without realizing it, I had bitten my lip. The metallic and salty taste of my blood reassured me. As if every cut finger that I had ever raised to my mouth and sucked on, had left a taste memory there, like a photograph of me that I could recognize. After feeling so afraid, the taste of my own blood acted like a soothing balm. I started to relax, breathe deeply, and loosen my grip on the oars.

As I recovered my composure, I happened to glance at the shore in time to see a dark shape lifting from the beach. It flew directly at me, at eye level. And, just as it seemed it would run right into me, there was a loud rush, a wide spreading of shadow that settled into form. A bird had landed on the end of my boat, landed so gently on the smallest space of decking and frame that the scull neither dipped nor rocked, not even in the slightest. Frozen: half out of confusion, half out of awe, I sat looking into the amber-ringed eye of a great blue heron. Wispy gray plumes of beard rustled in a breeze. Small rough sounds, hoarse whispered chirps and croaks slipped from the bird's throat while it cocked its head, pointing its long yellow spear of a bill slightly upward and in my direction as if to address me. I swallowed. The heron swallowed too, or at least something rose and fell down that long length of neck. Then as quickly as it had come, the heron left. With one powerful lift of its wings, it rose from the boat, made a cry so harsh and loud that I winced, and flew off down the beach.

Not more than a couple of seconds had passed, but the moment as I remember it was timeless. In the eye of that great bird, I glimpsed both emptiness and freedom. It would take another 10 years before I fully understood that the emptiness was within me, that no adventure, athletic pursuit, or professional identity could fill it. I would have to enter it, in order to find freedom from its haunting. But on that particular Sunday morning, I only knew what I saw in the heron's eye. It excited me, and unnerved me. I couldn't remember ever seeing an animal in such a way that I also felt somehow seen by it.

The heron a dark shape in the distance, my heart, as if stopped and then sparked gently back, made a small leap. My thoughts raced. *A great blue heron just landed on the end of my boat.* I was sure it was some sort of sign. I looked for someone, anyone who might also confirm this, but there was no one. Even the lady watering her pots had disappeared. *There will be marks in the decking* I thought, *evidence of what had happened.* With long powerful strokes, like the wing beats of the heron, I headed for the boathouse.

It seemed like such an extraordinary event to me. I wanted proof to verify it had occurred, but when I inspected the decking, there was not a mark anywhere. There was not one puncture or tear, no scratches or indentations. How could a bird that large leave no mark? I put my boat up on its rack still wondering.

Over the course of the next week, workouts tapered, boats were loaded onto trailers, and items on lists crossed off. Mostly, I put what had happened that Sunday morning behind me except that I found a little stone with a great blue heron figure painted on it. I purchased it immediately and carried it faithfully in my pocket. Finally the day came; I left Seattle and flew to Indiana for Nationals.

Standing on the shore of Eagle Creek Reservoir on a steamy overcast afternoon in June, I could not believe that I would be competing here, where I had grown up, in Indianapolis, Indiana. In the years that I had been away, my hometown had revitalized itself as the country's amateur sports hub. Along with housing many of the major governing bodies, it built facilities of Olympic caliber for swimming and diving, cycling and rowing. After all these years and traveling so far from this flat landscape of brown water creeks, cornfields, small forests, and pewter skies, it was as if I had traveled in a circle and ended up where I began.

Advancing through the heats easily, I made the finals in all four events that I had entered. The night before the finals, I lit a candle in my bedroom, my parents' guest room where I was staying. All the years that I had participated in sports, my folks had rarely seen me compete.

I used to feel sad about the fact, but now that they would see me rowing in the National Championships, my old disappointments melted away. Truthfully, I had not encouraged or asked them to come and see me compete until now. When I did finally ask them, they did not hesitate a moment before enthusiastically saying "Yes!" They hosted other rowers and put up the few members of our club in a motel by the reservoir. At the time I didn't realize how much I had kept them away from the events and feelings that were important to me by being vague or evasive, while I simultaneously longed for them to come close. This game that I played mostly without conscious awareness allowed me to perpetuate the myth that I was alone in the world, alone to carry both my dreams and my regrets.

Sitting quietly before the candle flame, I closed my eyes and envisioned each race, envisioned rowing well, pulling ahead, and crossing the finish line, first. I went to sleep confident, but awoke the next morning in a very different state.

The morning of the finals, the water was less than perfect. I cursed the weather as I carried my single to the launching area. I had rowed miserably in the pair race. Pulling too hard, trying to apply power where I needed finesse. Now a westerly breeze had risen and the surface of the water was rough. The single sculls event was the one that meant the most to me, the one for which I had trained the hardest. As I rowed to the starting line, I felt off and could not steady my balance both in the boat and in my head. Too many voices were telling me I was *worthless, no good*, that I would *lose*. While other voices would counter, the ones whispering their doubts were louder.

At the starting line I looked over at my competitors, women whose names I associated with greatness. I knew that I was gripping the oars too tight and my heart was pounding. I had rowed long enough to understand that I was defeating myself even before the command to "Row!" had been yelled. When it finally was given, I fell quickly behind and stayed in last place for the entire race. I felt mad when I came into the dock. Any hope that I had carried for an invitation to National Team Camp was surely gone now. All that work had been for nothing.

141

As I grumped about, refusing the encouragement of teammates, my mother came up to me. She said nothing, just put her arms around me. I could feel her love pouring into me. Then, she stepped back and said:

"Your dad and I are so proud of you. You were the only one in that race who had never rowed in a National Championship before. Two of those girls have been on the Olympic team." Then she smiled and kissed me on the cheek. "I better get back to your father. Have fun in this next one."

"Mom." She turned. "I love you."

She beamed and gave me a little wave, then went to be with my father.

"Have fun." Wasn't that what I always told the people I coached: to "row hard and have fun"? I started to feel lighter as my doubles partner and I took our oars down to the launching area.

When we went back for the boat, I said: "Terry, I'm sorry about the pair race. You did a good job calling it; I fucked us up by trying too hard and not rowing with you."

Terry looked at me with such warmth, a smile spread across her face. "Let's row well," she said.

"And have fun," I added.

That said, we launched our boat for the women's double sculls event. I don't remember much about the race except for our joint delight as we got off to a fast start and settled into a pace that felt almost effortless. Slowly but surely we pulled even with the third place boat and passed it easily.

"Cath," Terry yelled breathlessly from the bow, "we can take the next boat too. Pick it up."

And I did—quickening my hands, driving my legs harder while keeping the slide smooth. Terry, who was much shorter than me, answered. She lengthened her reach and quickened her hands.

"We've got 'em, I can see their stern," Terry yelled. "I can see the stroke, c'mon Cath."

Keep control, just pick it up. I moved everything a little harder, a little faster.

"There's the bow seat, we have 'em. Bring it up now—sprint."

I let everything go, every thought, and then we were flying. Not enough to catch the first place boat but enough to sail over the finish line for a silver medal.

"We did it!" Terry exclaimed, leaning over her oars and tousling my hair with a free hand. I laid back and looked at her grinning face.

"*We* did it, Ter," I said, emphasizing *we.*

Rowing slowly over to the medal dock, we bowed our heads as the officials placed silver medals on us. My dad and mom were standing nearby, waving and hugging each other. Some memories remain with me and that moment was one of them. I was, if only for a moment, a National Champion; not on my own, but with a partner much younger, smaller, and lighter, but someone whose spirit was large.

A couple of weeks later, I received a letter inviting me to a National Team Camp. It was an invitation that I had dreamed of, but one that I now declined. I knew that I did not have the drive to go any further. I was 34 years old. Through rowing I had found some healing. I learned that I could not do everything alone, but truly needed others. I had gained a greater measure of self-acceptance and the open approval and pride of my parents. I felt complete.

So many years later I can see how this pattern has played out in my life. I undertake something and follow it to its finish. While the finish is not always the one I imagine when I start—I know it, like the right answer, in my bones when it arrives. I held the letter to National Team Camp in my hands for a long time. Then, I refolded it and tucked it away in a journal. That fall I applied and was accepted into graduate school.

PART III

Falling in Love

It was early in October, the high Idaho summer was on the wane, and dry yellow leaves swirled in the occasional breeze. On the lake, a warm afternoon sun cut diamonds from the blue rippling surface. It was the kind of day I treasure, when the changing of a season can be palpably felt.

Walking across a dusty parking lot towards the main lodge of Hill's Resort, I felt excited about beginning my second year of graduate school with the Leadership Institute of Seattle. And although I had already spent a year in the program, I still marveled over the fact that school occurred in such a beautiful setting.

"Hey Cath!" The voice of my friend Sandy caught my attention. "Cath, wait."

Sandy was hurrying in my direction with another woman beside her, a woman I did not yet know but who would change my life.

"This is Dana," Sandy said, breathlessly introducing the other woman. "My cabin mate. She's an only child too," as if only children were an exotic or rare species.

Standing before me, with my very tall friend who'd been a college basketball star, was a shorter woman, with fair freckled skin and soft brown hair that just touched the shoulders of her starched white shirt.

She had a broad high forehead and stood with a straight and dignified posture while smiling with a common ease.

"Hi," I said, extending my hand. "I'm Cath."

Dana took my hand and smiled back, a little mischievously. "Guess I should have checked this morning to see what you were wearing."

Immediately I looked down, feeling self-conscious. We were dressed identically: both wearing the same brand of blue trousers that bloused in long lines from the hips and buttoned tight at the ankles, both wearing the same white shirts that were as crisp as the October air, and around our necks, we both wore silver necklaces. On Dana's hung a dolphin, on mine a labyrinth—the free spirit and the contemplative. I almost laughed but there was something uncanny about the coincidence. We didn't resemble one another physically: I was tall and dark; she was medium height, smaller boned, and fair. Yet when I looked at her, it was like looking into some kind of mirror. Even our eyes were similar—both brown, but where mine were dark, hers were flecked with gold, little flares lighting her smile.

In response to her comment, a line of heat moved up my neck.

"Nice to meet you," I said.

The woman standing in front of me smiled again, this time the warmth exploding across her face. Suddenly the air shimmered, exquisite and soft. Something passed between us, the way scent travels on the breeze; just when you apprehend it, it's gone. The sensation was so fleeting I couldn't be sure it happened, so powerful that I could not dismiss it. For a split second I felt a presence—if I were to name it now, I would call it a moment of grace. It was as if we were meeting in the presence of grace, a presence that was in us, surrounding us, emanating from us, and extending beyond us. Then as quickly as it appeared, it left, and I was aware that I hadn't really greeted Sandy and that school was beginning inside.

"C'mon," I said. "We'd better go." With that, I steered Sandy and

Dana through the double doors and into the main meeting room that was buzzing with introductions.

The Leadership Institute of Seattle, known by its acronym, LIOS, was a graduate training program for counselors and organizational consultants—a 2-year master's degree for mid-career adults. When I attended the program, it met six times a year for 7 long days, each time in various retreat settings. Classes began each day at 9:00 in the morning and lasted until 9:00 each night. As a laboratory educational process, LIOS was an emotionally, physically, and spiritually intense experience. When we practiced therapy, we practiced on each other; when we learned conflict mediation skills, we mediated the conflicts among us. It was a place where you could find endless support as well as endless challenge. It was also a place where people often came to know their classmates more intimately than their spouses, families, and friends.

That year, 1989, Dana was a first-year student and I, a second, and as a result we spent little time in class together. However, when we were not in class, we found ourselves in each other's company: sitting across from one another at meals, walking along the lakeshore during breaks, or talking into the wee hours of the morning after the day's curriculum was finished.

Quickly, we discovered that we could talk about anything. Although our initial conversations were about the ideas that we were studying or about our professional aspirations, we were, soon enough, unfolding the stories of our lives.

I found out that Dana had also been at The Evergreen State College in the early 1970s, and that she too had been a student of Willi Unsoeld. Her husband and I had even been in the same academic program there. When she said his name, I remembered him immediately: Mark, a tall blonde man with a ponytail and a passion for birds. After college, Dana told me, she and Mark had married, moved to Alaska, and homesteaded in the bush. They had two children, Kate and Alex. And, when Dana described running a dog team, hauling water, and doing diapers at 40-below—I realized I had met someone even more at home in the wilderness than me. Deciding to return to school for her master's degree, Dana had moved her family to Washington state or *outside* as Alaskans often refer to the lower 48. Now they were living along the Columbia River, along the Gorge. Dana described it as her "playground."

By the end of that first week, when we all said "goodbye" until our next intensive, I had a new best friend. Dana Elizabeth Illo. As we packed up our cars preparing to leave, she gave me a picture of herself. In the photograph Dana is standing alone, on a bluff overlooking the Columbia River. Her hands are thrust deep in her jean pockets and she's looking over her shoulder at the camera, as if beckoning. On the back she wrote in her calligrapher's hand: *Come play with me sometime.*

Midway through November, school reconvened. This time we met at a retreat center just east of Seattle. I was thrilled to see Dana again. During the opening meeting, I constantly looked at her from across the room. When she caught me staring, she would look quizzical as if to ask: "What?" I would shake my head or shrug my shoulders, smiling until she grinned and looked away. At the first break, I convinced another student to trade places with me so that I could sit beside her. I remember feeling so content in her presence that I could finally pay attention to what was being said in the front of the room. And so our friendship continued, with more walks, more conversations, and more time just hanging out together.

During that second module, after class one night I lounged in the hall with Dana, Sandy, and a small group of other women. As we pored over the events of the day, there was much laughter and a few tears—it's not easy to look at one's patterned beliefs and behaviors so intently. Eventually, exhaustion caught up with the conversation and one by one, the others filed away leaving only Dana and me. Since my room was in another building, a mile's walk down the road, we went to Dana's in order to keep talking.

Dana's room was located at the end of a long hall and looked out upon a small stand of Douglas fir. Even though it was well into November, she'd left the windows open—wide. When we walked in, the room was cold and smelled like a winter forest.

"Oh my God, it's one o'clock in the morning," Dana said, closing the windows. "Brrr—freezing." She rubbed her arms, then opened the closet and took a pillow and an extra blanket from its top shelf. Pulling the trundle bed from beneath her own, she began to make it up.

Earlier that evening, I had suggested that I could stay in her room, but now I felt uneasy. She seemed fine. She brushed her teeth and dressed for bed, still talking about something important from the day, but I was no longer listening. Even though I still had my hearing aids in, the room seemed very quiet. I began to undress. Electricity crackled through my short hair as I pulled my wool sweater over my head. Cool air touched my neck as I unwound my scarf, and as I unzipped my jeans, I could hear the little metallic grating sound of each tooth letting go.

On some level I knew that I was losing a battle with that part of me that had kept my heart guarded and my emotional life tidy and small. A new part was daring to emerge, a part of me that wanted more out of life, and was willing to risk losing that which was comfortable for that which was alive.

Climbing under the covers, I listened as Dana turned off the light. The dark settled like another cover over us while the scent of evergreen sifted about the room. Dana took a deep breath. When she let it out, it was as if she had been pondering something and had finally decided. She spoke softly.

"What really happened in your accident?"

People in my counseling program knew about the accident. It was no longer a secret, but neither was it something I talked about. Whenever it came up I brushed it off, as if it was simply a fact from my life, like being from Indiana or being Catholic. It was a story I skated over like a pond in winter, never touching what lay below.

In the years since, I have often witnessed how people who are engulfed by painful events avoid them. We bury them deep in our psyches, pile layer upon layer of defense over them so that the pain, and even the memories themselves, are all but forgotten, almost as if they never happened. It's uncanny too, how other people are inducted into our unconscious ruse and as a result never mention, confront, or inquire further into those painful parts of our pasts. So when Dana asked: "What really happened?" the question seemed suspended in the dark, as if she was handing me a shovel and inviting me to dig.

I wanted to tell the story to Dana, tell her in such a way that she would understand how enormously it lived inside of me, but how? Of all the people I had ever known, I believed she would listen and would be able to hear the things that I had never said. And yet, I could not imagine where to start.

"Just begin," Dana said, sensing my hesitancy.

So I went slowly, talking about camp, about Becky, about that fateful June morning. I told her about the way the sun rose round and orange, about struggling to stay awake, and finally failing. I told her how the Jeep rolled and Rita died. It seemed like I spoke for a long time, and when I finally stopped, a long sigh swept from me.

Dana reached down, and found my hand. "Seems like some part of *you* died that day."

It was a simple statement, but one that pulled me from my guarded perch into deep water. I struggled for breath. A part of me that had been forgotten started swimming for her life.

Dana eased down beside me and encircled me in her arms.

"It's OK, Cath," she whispered, "let it go."

She had barely said the words when I curled tightly against her. Big heaving sobs shook my body. I coughed and gulped for air and then cried harder. I lost all track of time as wave after wave of old pain pounded inside my chest. Dana simply held on. Finally, when the last of it was spent, she gave me a hug and opened her arms. I lifted my head and looked at her, trying to regain some sense of the present. She smoothed the hair from my wet face.

"It's about time you let that go," she said.

Then, as if this had been the most natural of occurrences—and I suppose to a mother used to soothing children and waiting out the storms of their hurts and fears, it was—Dana got up, changed her pajama top that I had wetted with tears, and returned to her own bed.

I don't remember thanking her, but I do remember thinking that she was right—I had carried the story for too long like an immense stone: guilt, remorse, rage, sorrow. Holding onto the story and all of its feelings had lidded my joy, my capacity for love, the courage to simply be myself. Dana was right: it was time to let it go.

As I settled into sleep that night, I had no idea how hard it would be to actually accomplish this, to truly lay down that which I had grown so accustomed to carrying. I had no idea how many times over the next 10 years I would revisit that morning, remembering it slowly, in small bits, until I could hold it whole. Over and over again, I would grieve what was lost until I could be glad for what was saved. I would curse my friends, my family, and God, until I could see my place in the larger human story, until I understood that no one passes through life untouched by its pain. I resisted the emotional work until resisting it wore me down and I found leaning into it, easier than leaning away. That night with Dana was the first step in what would be a very long walk.

The next morning I awoke refreshed. I felt like I had shed 50 pounds overnight. So profound was the feeling of lightness that I actually looked in the mirror, expecting to see my clothes hanging from my frame, but the woman who looked back was the same old me. Yet, I felt beautiful.

Slipping out of the building while Dana and the rest of the dorm were asleep, I raced up the road to the grocery to buy flowers. I wanted to give them to Dana; I wanted to give them to the world. I was happy and full, glowing with a warm blush like a woman who had stayed up all night making love. I was no virgin to sex, but when it came to intimacy: to the opening of my heart and the allowing of love from another to enter me and fill me, Dana was my first time. And when I went back to her room, I carried a bouquet of pink gladiolas.

After that second module, Dana and I spoke often on the phone. We also exchanged cards and letters regularly. Finally, early in December, I decided to take Dana up on her offer to come and play. I called Sandy, who I knew would want to come along, and together we made the 4-hour trip from Olympia to White Salmon where Dana and her family lived. It was late on a wet and blustery Friday night when we arrived at Dana's house. We met her husband, Mark, and her two beautiful children: Kate who was 8 and Alex who was 5; they were all on their way to bed. Dana, Sandy, and I did not stay up much longer ourselves since we planned to get up early and go hiking.

When morning came it was soft, gray, and calm. The kind of day that comes like a blessing after days of wind-driven rain, broken branches, and downed power lines. It was a morning when the air was still and the rain nothing more than gentle mist.

Dana, Sandy, and I headed out driving along the Columbia Gorge in Dana's old Volvo station wagon. The three of us talked non-stop while we sipped from big cups of steaming coffee. Since I was riding in the back, I occasionally missed pieces of the front seat conversation. Whenever that happened, I mused over the contents of Dana's car. Scattered in the far back were assorted tools, binoculars, bird books, and a few pieces of children's clothing. Beside me on the seat lay a lone tennis shoe and a stuffed animal, while psychology texts, journal articles, and plastic containers of unidentifiable leftovers lay on the floor. These were the artifacts from which Dana's life as a biologist's wife, a mother, a graduate student, and a commuter could be read like tea leaves. Taking it all in, I reconsidered my own tendency for order and neatness. *I am so damned tidy; maybe I should loosen up.*

"I'm taking you to my favorite place," Dana said as we drove along the Columbia River. Occasionally the gray sky would crack open and the sun would stream through, turning the water from a flat pewter color to that of liquid silver. It is the play of light upon water that makes the Northwest so magical: ever changing, ever mystical.

Before long we arrived at the trailhead. *Eagle Creek Trail* read the National Forest sign. After registering our names, we started walking. Quickly the lively chatter of the drive ceased and we fell silent. Surrounding us stood stately Douglas Firs and Western Red Cedars dripping and glistening in the mist. We had entered a great cathedral thick with the incense of decaying wood, evergreen spice, and rich earth. Nothing here is lost, I thought, simply buried beneath soft decay.

After a quarter mile, we stopped for water. Sandy kept her head down. Dana and I exchanged glances.

"Sandra, what's wrong?" Dana asked.

Sandy shook her head a little then looked up. There were tears in her eyes.

"I'm missing Mary," she said.

Sandy had recently separated from her lover and grief still filled her.

"You two go ahead," she said. "I just want to sit here for a while. I'll come along later."

"No, come with us," Dana urged.

I didn't say anything. I felt tender towards Sandy and respected her wish to be alone. I also knew that once she made a decision, she would not be talked out of it. And I would be lying if I didn't admit that the idea of being alone with Dana delighted me.

"C'mon, Sandy," Dana tried again.

"No. You two go ahead."

"You're sure?" I asked.

Sandy nodded, her eyes brimming. Dana reached out and hugged our friend. She always seems to know just what the other needs.

"Thanks, sweetie," Sandy said, slipping out of Dana's embrace. "You two go on now."

The three of us consulted our map and decided where and when we would meet up. Then, Dana and I left Sandy, sitting with her back to an ancient cedar.

Years later I would ask Sandy about that day. She denied that the high-intensity interest Dana and I were emitting towards one another shut her out. I'm not sure I believe her. I was crazy without knowing it, Dana too. We wrote letters to one another, talked almost every day on the phone, but each told ourselves we were just the best of friends. But that *best* friendship was a slow smoldering fire that was about to ignite and take both of our lives up in flames.

I followed Dana up the trail and once again the majesty of the forest lured us into silence. However, my mind was anything but quiet. It rocketed back and forth over its most favorite terrain: what might we do next, after our hike; what was happening in my current relationship, over which I was becoming increasingly hopeless; what was remarkable about my new friendship with Dana, who seemed like someone for whom I had been waiting all my life? I ask so many "what" questions, because I think if I can understand the details more clearly, the significance, the reason of a thing, then I can handle it. I never dreamed that I would know such affection for, or from, another. I couldn't imagine that I deserved as much. The thought, on more than one occasion, caused my eyes to fill.

"Water?"

Dana offered me an open plastic bottle. We had been climbing steadily and had stopped to shed a layer.

"Thanks," I said, handing the water bottle back. "This is an incredible forest."

"I know. Even though it's all second growth, it's still huge."

I felt so at home with this woman. Looking back it's obvious that I was attracted to her, but I was utterly convinced that we were merely good friends. I relied on the fact that she was married and had two children as evidence that nothing else was happening. Maybe I knew that if we admitted to anything more, we would be too frightened to continue and neither of us wanted to lose the other.

Now our deep woods trail joined a stream and slowly began climbing along its banks. All around us a symphony played and eventually, in the murmur of the mist, the sighs and whispers of the firs, the gurgle of the stream, I rediscovered my own rhythm. My mind quieted. The music pulled me inward and the beauty outward—like breathing.

Further on we arrived at an overlook. Below us what had been a clear running stream was now a tumbling torrent, crashing through a narrow canyon. The water turned and swirled, split between gray granite boulders, and then rushed to join itself again.

The trail finally brought us to the "punchbowl," a jade-colored pool in the bottom of a green velvet canyon, the stone walls thickly covered in mosses and lichens. At the head of the canyon, a 30-foot waterfall poured through a narrow opening and thundered into the punchbowl below. I cannot remember why but I decided to wade in, maybe for a better view of the falls.

I rolled up my pant legs and entered the swift moving water. The cold came like a hundred icy needles pricking my legs but the feeling was exhilarating, and when I turned, Dana was beside me. Years later she would tell me that when I waded out into the icy water that day, she knew she had a best friend for sure. We both are still known for our tendency to get in cold water.

We waded deeper out into the pool, taking each other's hand for balance while the waterfall came fully into view. Hundreds of gallons of water cascaded over a lip as narrow as on a pitcher; *what a journey water makes.*

Somewhere, high on the flanks of Mount Hood, a little seep issues from deep beneath the glacier. Silted and gray, the water runs like milk in rivulets across fields of broken rock until it converges in a shallow channel and that channel deepens into a bed. The bed winds down among the rocks and finally enters the forest. Now a stream, the flow hurries as if excited to be free. It tumbles along, losing the tiny pebbles and silicates that it has carried from above. Clear and green, it runs all the way to the edge of the cliff above us. There, without hesitation it launches into the air and falls crashing into the pool where we stand. And still from there it finds its way, rushing by us, back down the trail: past the overlook, past Sandy, past the great firs until it funnels into a culvert that carries it beneath the parking lot, under the interstate, where it launches itself one last time into the Columbia River. Water's is an ancient journey, a seemingly endless treading from mountain to sea, like our lives moving outward from birth, flowing through time to join again, the ocean of souls from whence we came.

I wanted to say all of this to Dana, but she already knew it. Why else would she have brought us here? We humans are mostly water—it flows through our own channels and streambeds, and along with air, gives life to our form.

"Wow!" I yelled to be heard above the roar. "This is beautiful."

"I know. It's my favorite place," Dana shouted back. "It's been a while since I was here, I mean to come more often..."

The rest of what she said was lost to me as she turned her gaze upward at the rim of the canyon. There was a softness about her eyes and her cheeks were rosy from the cold. There was a deep wisdom about this woman. I felt afraid. *What if I can't meet her?* Then a voice inside of me said: *Wade in.* I stepped further out into the pool. The water rose over my knees. Dana grinned and followed, taking my offered hand. We were facing the falls full on: the water soaking our pants, the wind and spray stinging our faces. Now it was Dana's turn; she took another step. I could feel the slightest pull upon my hand. In that moment I knew that she would never force me or push me—only lure me gently forward.

Together we stepped closer to the falls, holding hands. Since she was shorter than I, her steps had more serious consequences. Then she was in, almost to her waist. We both started laughing.

"We are crazy," she yelled. "It's freezing."

"No shit!" I shouted, smiling wildly. We stood together a moment more. My teeth began to chatter.

"Let's find Sandy and go get warm," she yelled.

We hurried back down the stream, almost running, no longer worried about keeping dry. Laughing and giggling, we delighted in how wonderful and silly we had been. When we arrived back at the overlook, we stopped.

"Let's go stand on that rock." Dana pointed to a large flat boulder jutting into the center of the stream. With a few quick moves, we were standing on her rock. The water ran before us in a smooth green tongue then burst into a series of white rooster tails and small waves. She faced me.

I have often wondered what it was we said that day, so many years ago, with only our brown eyes speaking? When we spoke without words, what was it we said?

In the weeks that followed our hike to Punch Bowl Falls and as the Christmas holidays drew closer, Dana and I could not keep ourselves apart; we talked on the phone every day, sometimes several times a day. Meanwhile, in sharp contrast, I distanced myself even further from my lover, Jan. I spent an increasing number of nights downstairs in my office, sleeping on a futon couch. I worked late when I didn't have to and declined Jan's invitations to play basketball—an activity that had marked us as a couple within our community for almost 7 years.

During this time I turned to my journal, covering its pages with thoughts, questions, and feelings. It seemed I was often tucked away, in the corner of some coffee shop madly scribbling, or sitting at my desk late at night writing by candlelight while the house, the neighborhood—the rest of my world slept. It was becoming increasingly clear that, while I loved Jan, I was no longer in love with her. There were so many things that were not working between us or at least that is what I wrote in my journal. Since I was looking for reasons to leave, it was easy to find them. I had changed in the last couple of years and wanted more: more emotional intimacy, more passion, more living than she and I seemed able to muster. The truth is I never gave her a chance. In reality I had already left, and given my heart to Dana. I felt both guilty and unfaithful.

One afternoon while I was at home studying and Jan was away at work, I became distracted, constantly looking at two pictures on my bulletin board: the one of Dana looking over her shoulder, and one of Jan I'd taken after a basketball game. She's sweaty, smiling broadly at the camera with a pair of basketball high-tops over her shoulder. I knew I had to choose.

The dozen steps from my office to the living room felt like a thousand; I sat down heavily on the couch. Across from me on the wall hung a framed poster of women playing basketball inside an old university field house. The light in the photograph was golden, casting the ancient wooden bleachers in shadow. Jan loved the game of basketball and played it with a passion. Through our relationship, I had come to love it as well. The framed poster was the one item in our house that we owned together.

I made my gaze soft and the women in the photograph began to move. I could hear the squeak of high-tops, the sound of heavy breathing and taut bodies bumping against one another. I could hear the bounce and the pass of the ball. It was a half-court game in progress that I was watching from the back of the gym. As I watched, I knew I would never play again. In my mind's eye, I saw one of the players turn; it was Jan, looking for me to move beneath the basket for her pass. I could tell by her face that she was confused by my absence. Then she turned her eyes to the basket rim and jumped for the shot. I could hear the ball ricochet off the backboard behind me as I walked out the door.

When the living room came back into focus, it was dark outside. Jan would be home soon. I would have to find the courage to tell her that our relationship was over.

A few days later, Dana showed up at our house. She was visiting another friend from our graduate program who also lived in Olympia. When I answered the door and saw her, my heart leapt, but when we hugged, I stiffened, feeling very self-conscious. I was now well aware that my attraction to Dana was serious, serious enough that I had decided to leave my relationship with Jan.

"Is everything OK?" Dana asked, concerned.

"I'm just distracted."

"What's up?"

"I don't know," which is what I say whenever I feel uncertain or uncomfortable. "Let's get out of here," I said. "Go for a walk or something."

Dana and I drove to a large wildlife sanctuary north of town—the Nisqually River delta. The day was bright, dry, and cold with a brisk wind running along the dike. As we walked, our feet shuffled through the last of autumn's leaves; we shuffled through our conversation as well. I kept to safe topics: Kate and Alex, how my thesis was coming. I longed to talk about what was happening for me; I was also very afraid. In the distance, a popping sound punctuated my thought.

"Shotgun," Dana remarked.

"How do you know?"

"I learned from Mark. On our first date he took me duck hunting." Dana stopped and struck a pose: tracking a line of imaginary ducks overhead with an imaginary gun tucked against her shoulder. When she had them in her sights, she squeezed the imaginary trigger and shrugged from the recoil. Her little pantomime made me laugh.

"You really hunt?"

"No, not anymore, but Mark still does."

Hunting was an abstract idea to me. While I could appreciate the skill it took, and think of a myriad of reasons why people would do it, I couldn't picture me actually shooting anything.

We hadn't gone much further when Dana stopped again; this time she knelt down. In the brown grass lay a dead female mallard. Dana stroked the duck's breast and then its head with amazing tenderness. There's a way Dana examines things that makes her strong hands seem smaller and more delicate. She presses her thumb against her first two fingers—the way one handles a fine teacup. This is how she touched the mallard; to me it seemed holy.

"She's not been dead long," Dana said. "See?" She opened one of the duck's wings and then folded it neatly back into place. "Not even stiff yet." Gently, Dana scooped up the duck and stood. "Give me your pack."

"What?"

"Open your pack. We'll take her with us."

"Why? What are we going to do with her?"

"Have her for dinner," Dana replied, looking curiously at me.

My face betrayed my astonishment. I couldn't believe I was going to carry a dead duck around for the next couple of hours, let alone carry it home and eat it. Dana tucked the mallard into the pack beside our thermos of tea and our raincoats.

"Here you go." She held out the pack for me. "Unless you want me to carry it."

I took the pack from her and we set out again. There was nothing about this woman that I did not like. She carried solid strength and childlike innocence. She was both compassionate and irreverent. I couldn't see how it could work, but I knew that I wanted to be beside her—for the rest of my life.

A few moments later it was I who stopped and turned to face her.

"I think we're having an affair of the heart," I said.

Now it was Dana's turn to look stunned.

"I am closer to you than I am to Jan," I blurted, "and I can't live with that betrayal any longer. It's not fair to Jan. I'm going to break up with her."

Dana inhaled sharply. Later she would tell me that she knew I was right and felt terrified at facing the implications. She too had been relying on the fact that she was married to protect her from admitting that she was in love with me. Perhaps since the day we met in that dusty parking lot, we had been moving towards this moment and doing everything we could not to face it.

"You sound sure," she said carefully.

"I am. Your friendship means the world to me."

I didn't say that I loved her. That would have been too much. Besides, it was obvious. Over the months of autumn, we had created a beautiful story about friendship and growing intimacy. Now, with the coming of winter we would have to face the truth.

Later that evening after our fresh duck dinner, Dana left and Jan and I sat down on the couch. After a while I told her I wanted out. She cried, as did I. We both knew the relationship was over and had been for some time. Still, the truth was painful to name. When we finally went to bed, we were exhausted. Yet, neither of us slept; we were too tired to talk anymore, too hurt to touch. The inches that separated us felt like miles, cold and hollow.

The next morning I met Dana for coffee; I told her what had happened. She seemed empathetic, but reserved.

"Take me with you," I said, tears sliding down my cheeks. She started to shake her head—no. "I'll take a bus back from Hood River." I was begging now. Feeling desperate. My life was starting to unravel and I had pulled the thread. I was terrified that she would walk away. Instead, she took me with her. I locked my car and left it in the coffee shop parking lot with no thought of when or how I would come back for it. Then, I climbed into Dana's Volvo and we headed south.

On our way to Hood River, Dana talked about her own marriage. She told me about the frustrations that both she and Mark had faced, the hurt and the anger that lay beneath the appearance of their loving family.

"I love my kids," she said, "and Mark is a great dad. We've created something special as a family, but between us—there's a wall. We live together, but very apart."

I believed Dana. She was not looking to hurt Mark, nor was she looking to use me. We had fallen in love, to both of our surprise and neither of us knew what the other would choose.

The rain fell steadily all the way to Portland. As we headed east on Interstate 84 along the Columbia River, the wind picked up as well. When we passed the turnoff to Punch Bowl Falls, I remembered how happy I had felt that day, a couple of weeks back, how innocent. Now all I felt was guilty and scared. We hardly spoke during that last hour of the drive, each of us lost in her own thoughts. There was no way to continue our friendship without hurting the people we loved. The closer we got to Hood River, the worse the weather. The wind thundered down the gorge in great gusts, blowing curtains of rain across the highway. More than once, Dana felt the Volvo, like her old life, beginning to plane. When she left me at the bus station, it was dark. I got home to Olympia after midnight, and when I walked into the house, I found a note on the kitchen table from Jan. She had left to stay with friends.

A week later, on the day after Christmas, I started looking for an apartment.

In that last week leading up to Christmas and in the week that followed, Dana and I did not talk. The tension between Mark and her had grown. Although she hadn't told him about us, he sensed something was wrong. When she finally called, on New Year's Eve, she told me all this and then she said, "I love you, Cath. I love you! Happy New Year's."

When I hung up the phone, I cried for a long time. No matter what happened, I knew that what was between us was real, not one-sided, not something I had made up. In that moment I believed that it was enough to feel that love given was also love returned. As the first hours of the New Year were born, I wrote in my journal by candlelight. On those pages, for the first time, I admitted that I wanted Dana, wanted to be her lover.

Several evenings later, I was sitting at my same old wooden desk, now tucked into the corner of my new apartment's living room. The small, one-bedroom unit on the second floor of a long "L" shaped building sat across from a shopping mall: not my idea of home, and certainly not a roomy space, yet I felt comforted living there, less constrained. I had quickly moved out of the house that Jan and I had shared and taken the first place I could find that was within my price range and close to my work. Looking back, I wince when I recall how sterile, ugly, and homogenous the place was and yet, at the time, I felt glad to have a place of my own, and blessed that the one fir tree in the parking lot stood outside my window.

I was sorting through data for my thesis when Dana appeared at my apartment door, blue rain jacket zipped with the hood up, dripping on the dingy hallway carpet with her unmistakably shining eyes. "I found you," was all she said.

My heart swayed like the fir outside. She had left Mark and the kids at home and driven the 4 hours to Olympia on a night full of rain and wind. I opened my arms to her and we hugged.

"Let me take your coat. Are you hungry?" I asked. "I have miso soup."

"No, but a cup of tea would be nice."

I went to the stove and began heating water. Dana went to my desk and started reading the top page of the thesis chapter I had just printed.

"There are some mistakes here."

"I know. I'm just trying to get the ideas out."

"How is it going?" she asked, taking the steaming mug of tea from me and seating herself on the futon couch.

I explained some of my findings, shared with her what I thought was of interest. When I finished she said, "That is interesting."

In spite of her response, Dana looked anything but interested. Her eyes traveled the room, taking it all in, as if deciding something.

"Mark's been sick." She said, "I'm afraid that Katie is going to follow. I shouldn't have come."

I took a deep breath, afraid of what she might say next.

"But I'm here."

"I know, thank you for coming." It seemed like such a small and frightened answer.

I put music on, warmed the soup while we talked more. The hours passed. Neither one of us wanted to make too much meaning out of the visit; yet neither of us could help but do so. Finally, tiredness dragged at us. We took turns in the bathroom. Although we'd undressed in front of one another before, there was a new shyness about us. She'd brought her pajamas and toothbrush, and although she had other friends in Olympia, she had come intending to stay the night with me. Still I felt cautious and offered a choice about sleeping.

"You can be out here, on the futon. Or, you can sleep with me."

Dana looked impatient. To this day she does not like it when I avoid saying what it is that I really want.

"Don't be silly." She picked up the candle that sat on the dining table and walked with it into the bedroom. I followed with my heart racing. I had dreamed of this moment a hundred times, the moment when I would feel her warmth beside me again.

Quietly, we slid under the wool blankets while the rain spattered the windows. Once again, the silence in the room was deafening. I tried to remain still, but my body buzzed as if a swarm of bees had been loosed within it.

In my memory, we rolled towards each other. The candlelight flickered and threw shadows dancing across the wall. I looked into her eyes, touched her face, and moved closer. Our lips gently found each other. The body knows how to give itself, if we only allow it. Meanwhile, the wind roared, the rain fell, and the candle burned low. Dana and I made love like a storm that had been a long time waiting.

What was it we said that day on the rock in the river? What was it we said before our eager coming togethers and reluctant leavings? What was it we said before "Yes" to a life together: to her children, a mortgage, to the soccer games and graduations, to the long and painful untangling of both our pasts? That day on that rock, what was it we said?

"I know you. I have always known you. And now, we will know each other once again."

Vashon Island

The first flush of Dana's and my love was also colored with heartache. We had been lovers for a year. She and her family had returned to their home in Alaska and I had moved to Vashon Island just across Puget Sound from Seattle. We still spoke almost daily and saw each other when Dana came into town for her second year of LIOS modules. How she, how any of them: Mark, Kate, Alex, endured those months, I will never know, but by February of 1991 the tension in Dana's marriage had become unbearable. Dana was reluctant to let go of the dream that all married couples share: that "I do" is a promise they can count on to the end of their lives, that their children will always know the love, guidance, and presence of both their mother and father. As for me, I was literally crazy in love. Looking back, I cannot believe how insensitive I was towards Mark and the children. In my right mind, I would have walked away from the affair, recognizing the pain it was causing. I was, however, completely lost in my love for this woman, so gentle and kind with a mischievous side that enjoyed being just a bit naughty, a trait that seemed a relief to me, me who always strove to be good. I loved everything about Dana and my blind love made it impossible for me to leave her side. One spring night the strain became too much for Dana to hold any longer.

The ferry to the Island was running late and we were sitting in the car, across the water, waiting. I could see the lights begin to blink off as houses on the far shore went to sleep. Dana had been quiet for some time. Then she spoke in a pained voice.

"Why can't we be a family—Mark my husband, you my lover?"

I wanted to answer, and even though Dana knew that the idea could never really be, I felt fearful of saying something wrong. Her very question threatened our relationship. If I forced a conflict, she might choose Mark and the kids over me. It was the very choice she didn't want to make and the one she could not avoid.

There were tears streaming down her face in the quiet of the front seat. "I'm going to Belize to be with them. I have to see if we can work it out."

Mark had taken Kate and Alex on a winter break trip to the Caribbean. Initially, Dana had stayed behind for school. Now she had decided to go.

I looked away, out the window, my own tears beginning, my face hot; some part of me believed that if she went, I would lose her.

"I will wait for you." My words surprised me.

"What?"

"I will wait for you," I paused, and then, "for the rest of my life."

In retrospect, my response sounds melodramatic, but in that moment I meant it with all my heart. I would wait, for Dana, for Dana and Mark to sort things out, for the kids to grow up, for Mark to die, whatever it would take for Dana to be free to return to our love. I simply could not imagine my life without her.

"If we have to, I will just be your friend." I meant that too, as I reached for her hand and with my other touched her cheek soft and wet with tears. I don't remember what Dana said in response, just the tired and tender way she leaned into me as we crossed the water to the Island.

The next morning Dana left for Belize and I kept busy: one minute telling myself that everything would work out, the next sure that we would never be lovers again. Each night as I crawled into bed, a bed that felt a little colder and less welcoming, I cried. I missed her voice or some word from her.

In the early days of our love, I didn't talk much to my friends about Dana. Some tried to talk me out of loving a woman who was married. "Affairs never work out," one said. "She'll leave you," said another. I did not want their protection. I wanted their loyalty, their support for the idea that Dana and I could make it as a couple. As I waited for some word from Belize, their comments haunted me. Then, finally, the phone rang. It was Dana.

"You wouldn't believe the dream I had last night," she said, after we had exchanged hellos and how are you(s)? The very sound of her voice soothed me.

"I was in a church, at a Mass," she related. "The priest had a huge bag of crystals, which he was giving out. But when he got to me, he only had a candle left. Then I woke up. And then, this morning, there was a procession through the town here, for the feast of Candlemas. All these people carrying candles walking to the church; I followed them and actually went to a beautiful Mass."

Dana saw the dream and what followed as a sign, our love full of light and crystals refracting rainbows. Mark had met a woman on the trip to Belize and was with her when Dana arrived. They never talked about their marriage, and now Dana was headed back to me. I felt exhilarated. When I hung up the phone I walked the beach by my house singing, smiling, re-imagining a life with Dana.

The following years would not be easy as Dana and Mark separated and eventually divorced. The *what ifs* and *I should haves* stayed with Dana for many years and sometimes still live like ghosts in her heart. Mark's anger and hurt eased and he moved to the Island to be close to his children. He remarried a wonderful woman of even temperament and brilliant mind, and together they adopted a daughter from Guatemala. Kate and Alex divided their time between our two households and after 7 years, we began spending our Thanksgivings and celebrating birthdays—together. Kate and Alex always knew they had a mother and a father who loved them. They gained two stepmothers who grew to love them too, and eventually a little sister as well. Our story did not turn out the way Dana first envisioned it and yet in some ways it did. Mark and Dana remained faithful to their children and Dana and I made a life together as lovers, and we are, all of us, family.

The summer after Dana graduated with her master's degree, she and the kids moved to the Island. I thought I was ready to create a life with her and Kate and Alex, but I was not prepared for its sacrifices and demands. I went from being the sole focus of Dana's attention, to a partner focused on settling the kids into their new life. I learned to cook waffles and put toys together by headlamp on Christmas Eve. I read stories aloud, attended baseball and soccer games, and intentionally got acquainted with the other parents on the sidelines. I learned the names of Kate's and Alex's friends and cleaned up after their slumber parties. I did what needed to be done, mostly with a great deal of joy. There were moments, though, in those first years when I wondered if I had made a mistake.

Late one Sunday morning in our third year together, friends picked up Kate and Alex to take them to a movie with their kids in Seattle. The thought of a whole afternoon alone with Dana made me giddy. Being alone together rarely happened anymore. I imagined us making love, maybe going for a walk or sitting by the fire.

Dana had gone upstairs to take a bath while I finished the breakfast dishes. And although she had seemed tired and distracted when she headed up, I was sure a bath would bring her back. I brewed a cup of tea to take to her.

"I made you a cup of tea." I stood happily in the doorway of the bathroom.

"Mmm, thank you."

I waited, looking at her pale skin glistening in the water, the windows steamy while a small votive beside the tub gave off a flickering light. Could she be any more beautiful? Longing to touch her, to move in close, I knelt beside the tub and stroked her shoulder. She flinched a little and pulled slightly away.

"What's the matter?"

"Nothing. I just want some alone time."

I removed my hand and she must have seen the hurt registering on my face.

"Can't I have some time to myself?"

"I'm sorry. I didn't know, I just thought maybe," I did not finish my sentence.

"I give everything," Dana said, "to make sure Kate and Alex are OK. I need you to understand that—they come first. I am just so tired; I just want to be alone."

"OK," I said loudly. "It's not like I don't worry about them. I do my part and I am tired too." The air in the room chilled between us. Dana was crying. I left not bothering to close the door.

Downstairs I paced, not knowing what to do. Then the phone rang; I answered it without thinking. It was my mother.

"Hi, honey."

"Mom?"

"Your father is watching football, so I thought I would call. What are you up to today?"

Normally, I would have given her a few facts and then asked if I could call her back in a while, but something compelled me to tell her the truth.

"Mom, I don't know if I can do this parent thing. I never have any time to do the things I used to, like hike or climb or even run. I'm always doing something for the kids or for Dana." I was whining. I wanted my mother to take my side, tell me she understood, and maybe suggest something that would help. But when she spoke, her voice was fierce in a way that I had rarely if ever heard.

"It was one thing when you were with Jan." My mother never used the words *lover* or *partner* when she referred to the women with whom I had been intimate.

"You could walk away from her with no strings attached, and you did—for Dana. Dana has children and they are now your responsibility too. So you better figure it out. It's not easy, but life never is."

Her words stung like a slap. Never had she spoken to me in that way. She continued:

"I thought you said Dana was different, that she was the one."

"She is."

"Then act like it."

My mother hung up on me. She had never done that either, not in all my years as her daughter. I felt hurt and mad. Mad because some part of me knew that she was right. Years later, I would remind my mother of this conversation, how fierce she had been with me. When she apologized for hurting my feelings, I stopped her and told her she had helped me more than she could ever know. Back then, though, I was not so ready to admit my fear or my selfishness, let alone accept responsibility for the choices I had made. After hanging up the phone, I took out my hearing aids, which I always did when I was angry. I put on my coat, a scarf, and hat, and walked out into the mist.

Dana, Kate, Alex, and I lived on the water then, in an old rented farmhouse. The place was always cold and drafty. When the wind blew hard, the windows rattled in their casings. The road out front meandered along the water on one side, along farms and woodlands on the other. That afternoon I walked and walked, crying and ranting. I was mad at my mother, mad at Dana, mad at Kate and Alex, mad that I had ever fallen in love—and I said so to the sky, the water, and the trees. After a while, though, I wore my anger out and just felt sad. I started thinking that I had made a mistake, that I was no good at relationships, that maybe I should leave. The truth is I couldn't leave, I was still crazy in love with Dana and living with Kate and Alex was amazing; they were making something of me that I could have never made of myself—someone better. My mother was right. There was no running away this time.

I was not far from our house when I passed a field anchored by a huge gray snag. The old tree had snapped in a storm and now stood dead and weathered the color of driftwood. It stood like a sentry as I passed. And, in a way, I had crossed a threshold of sorts. I could leave Dana, have other lovers, but I would always eventually arrive back at this place. To say "yes" fully to a relationship without the option of leaving tucked in my back pocket, tucked as a hedge against inevitable obstacles, was my crucible. I would never really know the price of love if I left. I would never grow up or grow beyond my fear of being left, my fear of not being strong enough to really love another, my fear of losing what I loved. When I arrived home, Dana was napping. Carefully, I crawled into bed beside her and fell asleep.

By hard work, love, and grace, we made it as a family. There were no maps for any of it. All the advice from parenting books, from therapists, from caring friends about how we should raise the kids and how Dana, Mark, his wife Nancy, Kate, Alex, and I should mend our lives into a whole cloth was just that: well-meaning advice, the best thinking at the time. Some of it helped, but most we discovered on our own through the daily living of our mutual lives. Mark never treated me with anything but respect and as the children have grown into flourishing adults, I am grateful for the resilience we all seem to carry and the patience with which we have loved.

VISITING THE GRAVES

Picking up my mother's car keys from the table in the hall, I left a note in their place and opened the front door quietly. Even though I was now in my forties, I felt 16 again, slipping out of my folks' house after they had gone to bed. Before I closed the front door, I glanced back at my mother, who had fallen asleep on the living room couch.

Curled in a purple silk robe on a large white sofa, she lay in a nest of brightly-colored pillows: turquoise, saffron, and lime. And although she was in her mid-sixties, there was something child-like about her face. Her mouth was slightly open as if she were about to speak, and all her usual lines and shadows had softened. Perhaps when we lay down our daily worries and surrender to the vulnerability of sleep, we unmask ourselves and regain, even if only for a few hours, some of our original innocence. My mother's young appearance stood in strange contrast to the way she now moved. On this visit, I had noticed for the first time how she steadied herself before entering an escalator or taking the first step at the top of a stairs. My father, nearing 70, had grown more careful as well. He shuffled as much as he walked and complained often of tiredness. Tonight he had gone to bed early.

"Like he does most nights," my mother commented worriedly as he disappeared into their bedroom before the last light had faded from the sky.

I was not ready to see my mother and father growing even older and frailer. The thought of one day having to make decisions about their health and well-being or move them from this house weighted me. They lived in a small brick condominium, in a gated neighborhood. This home was their sanctuary, a small white palace into which they retreated from the injustice and pain of the world like exiled royalty. White walls, white furniture, whitewashed floors, the starkness would be too much were it not for the vivid splashes of color everywhere: modern paintings, bright pillows, and plush rugs caught the eye and held it captive. Theirs was an ordered beauty of shiny surfaces and brilliant objects. It had always been that way. Our houses and apartments had seemed too beautiful for ordinary living; our family life, more an orchestrated performance than unfolding story. Aside from my father's strikes of rage, which as he aged became increasingly less frequent and less potent, the three of us lived as if we were afraid of fire. Anything that disrupted the order was quickly handled, suppressed, or omitted from the conversation. Our love was lived like a small flame: regulated, clean, and neatly contained.

I would like to claim that I am different from my parents, but I too treasure beauty, order, and calm. Cleaning house brings me pure pleasure, sitting quietly amidst candlelight and soft music brings comfort, and I love being surrounded by art. But I have also come to treasure the rest of my life, which is full of muddy boots, hurried departures, dishes in the sink, and laundry waiting in piles.

Looking at my mother's peaceful face, I felt a tug at my heart. Hers was the first face I had ever known and I her only child. For a time, she knew me better than I knew myself and I could count on her for comfort, guidance, and solace. But somewhere along the line, I stopped counting on her and began hiding from her. I kept my doubts, my frustrations, my anger and pain concealed. Some of that secretiveness was simply necessary in order to separate from her. Some was due to the belief that she could not witness my feelings without trying to fix or change them. And, some of it was due to my own reluctance—to disrupt the scripted orderliness of our family's life.

I started hiding my feelings from her in early adolescence, and eventually it hardened into habit. I loved my mother deeply and never doubted that she loved me equally as strong. And yet there was a gulf between us. Perhaps all daughters feel it; perhaps it is the price of womanhood. Still, I have wondered if by choosing to love women, I robbed my mother and me of something special. My lovers were my most cherished confidantes, confessors, and champions. Had I loved men, my mother might have maintained her role as the most important woman in my life. Closing the front door softly, I carried this well-acquainted ache into the night.

It was a cool and fresh June evening. An earlier thunderstorm had brought a hard rain that now dripped from the eaves, raced down the gutters, and lay in dark puddles on the street. As I drove to the video store to return the movie my mother and I had watched, I thought about this town where I had grown up, Indianapolis. It appeared much the way it always had to me, a conservative and quiet city, comprised of tree-lined streets, brick homes, and well-kept lawns. There were more strip-malls now, more sub-divisions and generalized sprawl, but the place still felt like small town surrounded by cornfields. Maybe it was the web of friends that I had made over 12 years of parochial school, sports, and camp. When I graduated from high school in 1973, one-quarter of the city's 600,000 residents were Roman Catholic; everyone knew someone in another parish. We all had friends across town, up north, and down south. Just driving to the movie store I passed a dozen recognizable homes, the houses of girls I had grown up with, gone to school with, and eventually left behind.

Winding my way down quiet back streets, my thoughts and memories came and went. Who I had been in high school, and who I had become 20 years later seemed in some ways so predictable. I was a youth of my time: a young woman who was socially conscious and eager to make a difference. I organized clean-ups, participated in protests against the war, played folk music on my guitar, and listened to rock on the radio. One of my high school teachers remembered me as "Not that good of a student, but a class leader. You inspired people and encouraged their dreams. And, you were kind to everyone," she had said. Over the years my idealism waned, but not my faith in people. When

I lost faith in myself, I never lost it in others.

Going *home* always means encountering the past, with all its attendant feelings: painful, sentimental, confusing. All the memories and unfinished business wait like prying relatives at the gate when we arrive at the airport, the bus station, or front door. Over the last 20 years, I had traveled back to Indianapolis only twice, managing instead to meet my mom and dad in various other locales for our visits. It was my way of avoiding those relatives. But this visit was different. It was the past, specifically, that I had come to visit. I had come back to Indianapolis to visit Mrs. Ernstes, Rita's mother, who I had not seen since Rita's funeral.

Recently, I had started seeing a therapist, something I had done on and off since entering graduate school a few years earlier. I was drawn to the process, but never stayed with it long enough to make much change. I felt as if I was two different people: one who met the outside world every day with optimism and confidence, to whom others looked for inspiration and support; another who remained imprisoned within, young, hurt, angry, and afraid. In my dreams, I often saw a young girl standing outside the entrance to a cave. That cave lay within me, and the part of me that I would not allow out lived in its depths. Over the years, I became both drawn to this cave and terrified of what I might find inside. Therapy had helped me putter about its entrance, turn over some important stones. But it had not yet helped me find the courage to go in.

"You have never seen Rita's mother since the funeral?" my therapist had asked, unable to hide her incredulity.

"No," I responded, flushing, first with shame and then anger.

"How do you feel about that?"

I wanted to say, *Well, it's clear how you feel about it,* but I didn't. I had spent many years managing my feelings and protecting my vulnerability. I could conceal and bury an honest reaction almost immediately. I was so good at this that I often fooled myself as well as those around me. Calmly, I agreed with my therapist, and added that I thought it was probably time to go back and make the visit. We spent the next month of sessions rehearsing for the trip, turning over little stones while wandering further from the cave.

But now I was here, in Indianapolis, with only 2 days left in my visit and I still hadn't called Rita's mother. It's not too late, I thought as I dropped the movie in the big, blue return box and started to pull away. A lighted phone booth stood at the end of the parking lot. It's moments like these that make my own life seem like a movie, or maybe that's just the way I rationalize the synchronous appearances of help. Without daring to think any further, knowing I might bail out, I pulled over to the booth.

Once inside that box of glass, the world narrowed. The glare from the overhead light made the booth stuffy. It smelled of old urine, cheap wine, and spoiled milk. Someone had written a phone number and drawn a penis in red lipstick on one side of the glass while a BB shot had shattered the other side into a spidery web of fracture lines. A wad of gum was stuck to the phone itself and a mangled book of yellow pages dangled lifelessly below. The ruin of the place, its harsh lighting and awful stench, was vulgar and depressing. Maybe it mirrored an aspect of myself. One of the ways I kept my feelings managed was by holding them with a similar disdain, disrespect, and contempt. I was not conscious of this at the time, nor was I very thoughtful about the call I was about to make. I had said I wanted to do it and now I simply wanted to get it over with.

Pulling a scrap of paper with Mrs. Ernstes' phone number from my pocket, I dialed. Written in pencil, it was smudged from all the folding and unfolding over the course of my visit. I had carried that slip of paper everywhere: transferring it from one pocket to the next, from wallet to address book. Each night as I lay down to sleep, I slipped it beneath my pillow. By protecting it, I protected my heart. I did not want my folks to know what I was up to; I did not want to feel like I had to explain or reassure them. It was all I could do to reassure myself.

"Hello?" a warm voice answered. Immediately, I knew it was Rita's mother—not by what I heard with my ears, that was simply the voice of any older woman. I recognized this voice in my bones, as if the vibration of it touched me the way her hand had once, on my shoulder in the emergency room. If a moment ago, I felt solid and firm, I now felt as if I was dissolving. I gripped the receiver, willing its black plastic hardness into me.

"Hello?" Mrs. Ernstes spoke again.

"Uh," I cleared my throat, "Mrs. Ernstes?" I asked even though I was sure it was she.

"Yes. Who's this?"

"Catherine, uh, Cathy Johnson." She would not know me by my formal name; she only knew the younger me.

"Oh my land."

In the pause that followed, my breath blew like a long cold whisper across my lips. What was she thinking? What was she remembering? My mind flooded with the possibilities. I closed my eyes and pressed my forehead against the glass.

"Are you in Washington?"

Her question, innocent and understandable, brought me back to the present.

"No, I'm here in Indianapolis, visiting my folks."

"How are they?"

"They're fine. Fine," I repeated a little too loudly, afraid of losing the moment and my resolve. What I said next flew out of me.

"Mrs. Ernstes, can I come by and say hello—tomorrow?" A thousand synapses fired at once, a spate of memories and thoughts filled the small space between the intake of her breath and the exhale of her answer.

"Why of course, of course."

There had been so many times when I thought that Rita's mother and whole family must hate me. I knew in that moment it was simply not true and never had been. I wanted it to be true, though, because it would make the pain easier to bear if someone else was inflicting it. But, it was me who could not forgive myself. Long after everyone else had said that it was just an accident, I was still bearing the fault.

"Would afternoon be alright?"

"Afternoon would be fine. I'm watching Ceil's kids tomorrow but that won't matter. Come any time."

I must have been in shock, because I finished the conversation, hung up the phone, got in the car, stopped by a liquor store, bought some beer, and drove out to a gravel quarry we had frequented as kids. I did all this without thinking or feeling a thing. It was only while sitting in the quarry's darkness with my back against the front grill of the car, a beer in my hand, that my thoughts began registering again. I had done it. I had finally called Rita's mother and she had sounded glad to hear from me. I felt relieved, but there was something else looming inside of me, something too big to approach out here alone.

Years later, I would try therapy again. This time, I would stay with the process. I would remember more of what had actually happened during the accident and more importantly, experience the feelings that I could not when it had occurred. Those feelings were the thing too big to approach that night at the quarry. As the warmth of the engine at my back kept the chill of the night air from seeping into me, a chorus of frogs began. I closed my eyes and listened to their song.

The next afternoon I pulled up in front of the Ernstes' house, a wood and brick two-story, with a front porch that I had seen a thousand times in my mind. I felt anxious as if this were a first date or a job interview. Earlier that morning I had called home, to the Island. Dana had answered the phone sleepily.

"Hi, honey. What's up?"

The sound of her voice cut through my defenses. I got up from the kitchen table, carrying the phone with me, and went outside so we could be alone.

"I called Rita's mom last night."

"Oh, sweetheart."

Her voice sounded quickly more awake. I could hear something rustling and imagined her getting out of bed. I could see her in her faded flower pajamas walking into the kitchen and beginning the coffee, looking for the milk pitcher among last night's dishes still in the sink. I missed her warmth and the security of our routines. I picked up a small rock and held it in my hand as we talked.

"It wasn't as bad as I thought it would be. Mrs. Ernstes sounded glad to hear from me. I'm going over to her house in a couple of hours."

"I am so proud of you."

For much of my life, I had felt alone, staying guarded—keeping others, even my lovers, just slightly away. Dana was the first person I had allowed to come truly close. I started to cry.

"Honey? Talk to me."

"I don't know," I said, gulping and sniffling. "I don't know if I can do this."

"You don't have to, you know?" She waited a moment and then said more softly, "Cath, you have wanted to do this for a long time, it's a huge step."

"I know," I said, wiping tears and snot from my nose with the back of my hand. "I know." Dana had, from the start of our relationship, been able to see past the walls I put up. The first time she had hugged me, she later said, she felt my body stiffen. But my resistance gave way in the face of her gentle persistence.

Falling in love with Dana was the first opening. If I were to love her, I would also have to face losing her. The accident and Rita's death had left me feeling broken and lost, believing that I would surely lose, or that God would take from me, anything or anyone I dared to really love. I also believed that if such a loss occurred again, I would not survive. By loving Dana, Kate, and Alex, I was risking everything once again.

"Would you tell me you love me?"

"Oh, Cath," she said, and then with the tenderness that has marked our affection from the start, she continued, "I love you so much…"

The way she says it, the sentence sounds unfinished as if she is looking for another way to express what she feels. The space this leaves is warm and generous. That morning I wrapped her words, her voice, our life together around me like a blanket, and I could still feel its comfort as I walked up the steps to Rita's house.

Mrs. Ernstes appeared at the screen door, as large and jolly as I remembered her from high school. Her once fair hair had grayed, completely; she wore a flowered housedress.

"Cathy Johnson. Come in."

I stepped into her living room like it was yesterday. I wanted to take it all in, maybe sit quietly, but Mrs. Ernstes was offering me iced tea, telling me that she had called Claire who just lived down the street and would be over any minute. My feelings couldn't catch up, everything started happening so fast. Charlie Ernstes, Rita's little brother, was getting up off the couch to shake my hand. He ended up giving me a hug instead. As he did, Claire burst through the door with two kids in tow. The conversation turned chaotic—everyone talking at once, asking questions, correcting each other's information and memory the way large families do.

"Have you seen Becky lately?" Mrs. Ernstes asked.

"Cathy doesn't live in Olympia anymore," Claire corrected her mother.

"Where do you live?" asked Charlie.

"I live on an island near Seattle," I answered looking at Charlie, then turning to Mrs. Ernstes, "I don't get to Olympia very often." What I did not say was how uncomfortable it was for me to spend time with Becky.

I was living in Tacoma when Becky moved to Olympia. And although I would see her in later years at basketball games, and occasionally in the same social settings, I steered clear of too much interaction. Being with her made me feel incredibly uncomfortable. She was a living reminder of something I wanted to forget. Whenever I was with her, everything unspoken between us sat like a third person in the room, someone mute and invisible to her, someone yelling non-stop at me.

The Ernstes family and I continued catching up, establishing common and current points of reference: the names of children, our various occupations and hobbies, the similarities between Seattle and Indianapolis. All the while I kept looking for an opening, a graceful way to bring up the accident and Rita's death.

Above me, on the front room wall, hung the senior photographs of all the Ernstes children, framed 8x10, black and white studio portraits. The six girls wore either a black sweater or a black drape that just covered the shoulders and fell with a modest "v" over the bosom. Charlie wore a dark suit coat, white shirt, and solid tie. The only variation in the gallery was Rita's; there was no photograph of her. Instead, there was a pastel portrait that someone had made to resemble a senior picture. I have no idea why there was no photograph of Rita, but the fact that there wasn't contributed to my anxiety and my guilt. It was as if I had been the thief, who had stolen into their lives and taken the photograph of Rita with me.

The visit rolled on, into its second hour and second glass of iced tea. The afternoon heat increased, so Charlie found a fan that swung back and forth, sending a little breeze across our legs. Claire's little ones began to tire and complain loudly. I too felt weary, my courage melting. Before I knew it I was standing up, saying that I was running late for an appointment that I truthfully did not have. I promised to stay in better touch, we all hugged, and then it was over. I got into the car, turned the air conditioner on high, and drove back to my parents' house.

I felt as flat as the late afternoon light. High clouds had rolled in and the air was growing still. Thunderheads were building in the west. I wished some storm would blow through me, and once and for all tear off the roof of shame and level the house of guilt that I had built. I could not believe that I had come this far, after all these years, and accomplished nothing.

I know now how unrealistic my expectations had been. To think that I could simply walk up onto the porch and into the front room of Rita's house some 20 years after her death, having had no contact with her family and very little experience talking about the accident, even less about my feelings, and then have such a conversation with her mother, now seems incredibly naïve. Years later, I would understand how much I needed to talk about what happened, to tell the story again and again, to hear others' version of that same story, and cry until the crying was complete. That afternoon, I only knew that I felt heavy like the weather, disappointed over what I saw as my failure to confront the past.

The three of us spent our last evening together talking about my father's business, about their plans to go to New York in the fall, and fantasies about moving to the Northwest to live closer to me. I participated in this conversation with some sadness. I had just done something large in the life of my soul, but could not find the necessary courage to tell the two people who had shepherded that soul into this world.

The next morning my mother and I left early for the airport. Rather than take the typical interstate route, I drove us through town. My mother chatted warmly next to me in the front seat.

"Your Aunt Gracie is very interested in the lay ministry. She's writing a column..."

"Mom," I interrupted.

I could tell by my mother's expression and by the way she was sitting with her hands folded in her lap, looking at me with wide eyes, that she had been frightened by my tone. I gentled my voice.

"Mom, I want to visit Rita Ernstes' grave."

Her eyes moistened.

"OK," she said, her voice sounding a little wary.

St. Joseph's Cemetery was on the way to the airport, at least on the way that I had selected to take us. My mother and I rode in silence. I felt guilty for interrupting her story about my aunt.

"I just want to see her grave," I explained in defense.

My mother nodded and turned slightly as if to look out the window.

I do not give my mother enough credit for the ways in which she knows me. Perhaps the reason for my visit was not a secret to her; when I was younger, she could always see through my ruses and my lies. Maybe it was an illusion that I had distanced myself from her. Maybe I had only stopped talking explicitly about the things that were important. Maybe she, who had once carried me and known my every mood, could still feel when I was sad or lost.

We turned off a busy boulevard, passed through the gates of St. Joseph's Cemetery, and wound our way up to the chapel and main office. On either side of the drive were green lawns, and row upon row of stones and crosses. It struck me as odd that I had not come here before, but I could not think why I would feel that way. At the office, I asked for the location of Rita's grave while my mother stood quietly beside me. An older gentleman, with thin gray hair and half glasses perched on the end of his nose, the only person visible in the office, helped us. His liver-spotted hands shook just a little as he unfolded a cemetery map and explained in a voice that was quiet and yet surprisingly full how to find Rita's grave. As he did, he drew on the map with small neat arrows that would guide us.

"Thank you," I said and turned to go. Then I heard my mother's voice behind me.

"I would like to know the location of Catherine Rembusch's grave."

It was my turn to look with wide eyes. Catherine Rembusch was my mother's mother who had died of tuberculosis when my mother was 12. My mother had never been to her own mother's grave, not once in almost 50 years. Perhaps that is why it struck me as odd that I hadn't been here: my grandmother and namesake was also buried here.

We visited Catherine's grave first. The midday sun was hot; there was little shade and not much breeze. My mother and I stood perspiring before a simple stone, one in a small family plot that now holds my grandfather and his second wife as well. Quietly we looked at the name and the dates as if we could pass through those letters and numbers and meet again the person we missed. Every now and then, my mother's lips moved as if she was praying or talking to someone: maybe herself, or maybe her mother. How far back was she traveling? What words might she be saying?

I felt as if I should do something or say something. Slowly, I stopped watching my mother and focused on Catherine's name on the stone.

Hi. It's me, Catherine, your granddaughter. Can you hear me? I listened for an answer. Nothing. I didn't feel disappointed though. Instead, I felt strangely at ease, yet strong. The colors of the day seemed more vibrant. I felt no need to hurry, to do or say anything. I waited while my mom spent time with hers.

When my mother seemed ready, though I think she could have stayed longer and know that she went back since, we drove to the area of the cemetery where Rita's grave was located. All the stones in this section were small and flat rectangles that lay like pavers on top of the grass. We walked by half a dozen, then past a large maple tree that offered much needed shade and then found the stone for which we were looking.

Rita J. Ernstes. 1955-1973.

Name and date, nothing else. Suddenly I wished that I had brought flowers, though there were very few graves in that section that had any. Everything seemed tidy and quiet. Was anybody really here? A heavy feeling settled in my legs.

"At least she gets some shade," I said, trying for lightness, afraid of the pressure that was building behind my eyes. The ease at Catherine's grave gone, I now felt self-conscious with my mother standing beside me. My feelings and thoughts about all this had been so private, known only to me for so long that letting her witness them was painful. A little breeze stirred. My eyes filled. I bit on my lip to keep from sobbing. Then, my mother's hand was on my arm.

"Does it hurt much?" she asked.

I am not sure what I believed at the time, but looking back I can see how courageous was her question. In her own way she was attempting to bridge the 20-year lapse of silence between us. I wish I'd understood that then. I wish I would have cried, telling her everything: how frightened I had been, how sad, how incredibly sorry. I believe she would have listened, understood, and comforted me. But I said none of this; instead I put my arm around her shoulder, noticing again how small and frail she was becoming, and answered:

"Sometimes."

An hour later, I looked out my window as my flight home to Seattle climbed higher into the sky. I watched as the farmlands below grew smaller and smaller until they were nothing more than a quilt of green and brown. I had been born there, in a land of good soil and hardwood forest and it was as if from that land I had learned a soft heart and a strong stand. The engines throttled back and the jet slowly banked westward. I took out a piece of stationery and a pen.

Dear Mrs. Ernstes, I began. *Not a day goes by when I do not think about Rita and what happened on the day of her death.*

I mailed the letter, but never received a response. Seven more years would pass before I would return to Indianapolis, and when I did, I carried flowers for Rita's grave.

The Sound of Grace

...in all faces
the Face of faces
is veiled as a riddle
– Nicholas of Cusa, fifteenth-century Christian mystic

In 1999 Kate graduated from high school. Dana and I gifted her with a trip to Paris. Those days together were magical; we walked everywhere, crossing back and forth over the Seine, visiting museums and gardens, sipping espressos at sidewalk cafés, lingering in small shops for what seemed like hours. One, I remember, sold expensive stationery and fountain pens, a letter writer's dream.

Finally it came time to say goodbye. Kate had made plans to travel on for the rest of the summer with a childhood friend. We hugged tight.

"Have a great time, have fun." I could feel my eyes brimming. "Be careful."

"We will." She slipped from my arms, gave her mom a big hug, and walked away. Watching her go, I saw both the little girl and the stunning young woman she had become. My heart ached for her beauty, her grace and athleticism, for all that lay ahead for her. I whispered a prayer: "May it be good."

Dana and I also traveled on, to the south of France: first to the Pyrenees and then through Provence. The slow pace of the French countryside suited us. I have a photo from that time, of Dana sitting at an outside table looking into the distance. The sun must be setting, because her face is bathed in warm yellow light. She is beautiful.

Before we flew home we enjoyed one last afternoon in Paris, one that I will never forget.

I paused at the top of a steep concrete stairwell that led down to the underground world of the city's Metro. I removed my hearing aids, anticipating the overwhelming sounds that lay ahead. Instantly, the traffic and the conversations around me blurred and receded. The iron handrail I grasped felt hot where the sun rested on it. A little breath of breeze brushed through my hair, and something savory drifted from a café next door. Because it was our last afternoon in that enchanting city, I wanted to remember everything—even the pull of people: young and old, tourist and Parisian, flowing by me, descending the steps, and vanishing into the shadows below. I stood there at the top of those stairs, listening for a few more moments, taking it all in. Then I, too, headed down to the trains.

While the tunnels of the Metro provided instant relief from the city's summer heat, they assaulted the senses in other ways. Fluorescent light glared against white-tiled walls only to be swallowed by winding miles of concrete and darkness. The place was both too bright and depressingly dim. A deep breath uncovered the fruity smell and acrid taste of axle grease, perspiration, and urine. And every few minutes, the air swelled with the roar and vibration of an arriving or departing train.

Shuffling forward with my ticket, I could hear the thunk, thunk of turnstiles ahead, but there was another sound as well. A few errant notes of music filtered above the chatter and hum of the moving crowd. As I passed through the turnstile and headed for the train that would carry me to the Louvre, the crowd thinned but the music remained, growing louder and more pure. Long and soulful tones were rising and falling, reminding me of someone crying out for pure pleasure and then weeping gratefully in such pleasure's wake. The voice of a single violin imbued that tunnel with grace.

I do not remember walking the rest of the way to the platform that day, only how the music inhabited me. Each draw of the bow made me large, each return across the strings, small. A distance that could have only taken a few seconds to cover became a pilgrimage. Deep sorrow and deep gladness moved through me, as if I had been away from one I loved and had returned home at last. Finally, I reached the source of the music: a middle-aged man sitting on a folding aluminum campstool with an open violin case at his feet.

He was heavy in the belly, but sat on his stool with a straight back, as if occupying a principal chair with the symphony. His hair was pulled into a scraggly gray ponytail and his dark flannel trousers were worn, frayed at the cuff and along the seams. The sweat stains that darkened his light blue shirt belied the otherwise invisible effort with which he played. I stared, unable to look away. Not only was I hearing the music—it poured in through my eyes. Each line shimmered brighter, the pitch building and straining, like the sounds of a lover well loved. The music was so pure that the fibrous strings of my own heart began to vibrate and break. And in that moment, standing on the platform slightly apart from the crowd, I knew something of God, and God knew again the incandescent instant when suffering ceases, could feel the breaking of a thankful heart.

With tears streaming down my cheeks, I searched the musician's pale round face, hoping for his gaze. In the presence of such grace, I could not bear to be alone. Surely he will understand, I thought. But when my eyes finally found his, they were half closed and empty—the wandering white oceans of the blind. I have thought many times since how the voice of God spoke that afternoon to a woman hard of hearing through the hands of a man without sight.

HEALERS

Over the course of 30 years I have wondered, over and over, how my life would have been different had I had someone to help me through the tangle of feelings, painful memories, and punishing thoughts with which I was left following the accident. Early on, I adopted the belief that I had been shortchanged: abandoned by my parents, my teachers, my friends, by God. While I can see how I came to that conclusion, I can also see that it was not true. I was not abandoned. It was the times, the way my family dealt with loss, my own personal difficulty with knowing how to ask for help that collided and led to my quiet exile. With the grace of years, I can see that all along the way there were people who helped me, people whose mere presence in my life called me to come more fully home. By *home* I mean that space in my heart where acceptance, forgiveness, and gratitude flourish; where I am at peace and feel truly grateful for the life I have been given. When I was finally ready, two particular healers appeared in my life to help me take those last steps—home.

It was my dentist who referred me to Dr. Corinne Bell, an Osteopath whose specialty was Obstetrics and Gynecology but whose gift to me was her skill at craniosacral therapy. The dentist thought Dr. Bell might be able to relieve the tension in my jaw that was severely affecting my bite. For years I had suffered from a chronically stiff neck, a ridiculous bite (no two teeth in my mouth actually meet correctly), and a jaw that popped every time I opened "wide." Some of my bottom teeth were cracking from the pointed pressure of that misaligned bite. Having lived with the symptoms for so long, I couldn't imagine feeling any different, but at age 45, I wanted to do what I could to preserve my original teeth. So on my dentist's advice, I called Dr. Bell and made an appointment.

Dr. Bell's receptionist showed me into a richly paneled office. One wall was lined with medical textbooks, on the other wall hung a large canvas, an English garden scene bathed in soft light; behind me a set of bay windows opened across Puget Sound and into the heart of the Olympic Mountains. I sat down in one of two soft leather chairs facing a large, dark wooden desk and waited for Dr. Bell. In a few minutes, a small woman with short blonde hair and pale blue eyes wearing a white lab coat emerged from an examining room and introduced herself as Corinne Bell. After shaking my hand with a firm grip, she seated herself across from me behind the desk and opened my medical history.

"Compound fractured jaw from an automobile accident," Dr. Bell read from the history. "Did you hit the steering wheel?"

I nodded.

"Is that the scar?" She tilted her head, eyeing my face, squinting to get a better look.

I lifted my chin and turned my head slightly to the left, so the small patch of dark thickened skin that lay along the line of my jaw was more visible.

"Severe concussion, soft tissue injuries to the face, shoulders, and chest… sounds bad."

Cold crept through my core. I wanted to look away, but there was something about Dr. Bell's gaze that held me. Maybe she could see that part of me was preparing to run.

"Were others with you?"

Her tone was matter of fact and conversational. She could have been inquiring whether I'd had the measles or chicken pox as a child.

"Yes." I focused on her blue eyes; they seemed so kind. Still I shivered. "There were four others." She nodded.

I will always wonder what led her to ask the next question. Maybe she could see some sadness in my eyes or wondered about the forward round of my shoulders. A body worker once told me that I carried myself like someone burdened.

"Was anybody killed?"

It was such a simple question, but one that I had never had to answer. My mouth went completely dry and my body turned to stone. I had been waiting all my life for someone to ask that very question. I wanted someone to see into me, to see what was so distressing for me to reveal. Like a character in a fairy tale, I had been a prisoner inside a tower of my own creation. And Dr. Bell with her simple question was opening the tower door.

"Yes," I answered, barely audible. "Her name was Rita."

A great expanse of silence seemed to spread between us. Yet, Dr. Bell's eyes never left me. I thought I saw the beginnings of a tear, but she blinked and it was gone.

Slowly, Dr. Bell pushed back from her desk and stood up. She looked down once more at my chart, gave a determined sigh, and then fixed me with a strong gaze.

"If I treat you, you will have to face what happened."

A wall of defiance rose in me. *What does she think? Does she think this is news to me? I have lived with this story for nearly 30 years—what's to face?* "I'm not afraid to cry in front of you," I said, a thread of arrogance in my voice.

"OK. Then let's have you up on the table."

Dr. Bell made a few manual adjustments to my hips and pelvis; then she slid her hands beneath my back. Immediately my eyes closed. I could not have held them open if I had tried. Dr. Bell's hands warmed. As she moved them slowly along my spine, they grew hot. I remember wondering how hot they might get when a wave of great intensity started to build within me. It was as if all the mass of my being was drawing up inside my skull the way a straw draws water from a glass. My heart started beating faster. I felt like I was on a roller coaster inching its way to the top of the steepest drop on the ride, and the exposure took my breath away.

"Keep breathing," Dr. Bell directed. I exhaled and then inhaled. And if breathing were a way through the dark, I was now hurrying towards the light. My back arched off the examining table and the top of my head felt as if it would explode. Then, as intensely as the wave had built, it ripped out like a flood. It shot down the length of me, and banged against the soles of my feet in one convulsive shudder.

"Good," Dr. Bell said. "That's good. Just lay there and rest."

A deep peace settled over me. It was summer and I was floating on a raft. Overhead a blue sky opened, the blueness growing, washing over my entire view. A sweet oily smell wafted by; I became aware of something scratching. Opening my eyes, the sky was replaced by Dr. Bell's paneled office. She sat at her desk, head bent, writing notes in my chart; the scratching sound was the nib of her pen. I closed my eyes again and the blue returned. The view seemed familiar, but from where? Then it came to me: I recalled the morning of the accident, unable to move and focusing on the sky. This, I thought, is a scene from the accident, but in that moment it was more than a memory. It was as if I were once again there. I had no other thoughts or feelings, just physical sensations, but I knew exactly where I was: the shoulder of the interstate. So real was the experience that I opened my eyes to check that I was still in Dr. Bell's office. I was and Dr. Bell was still at her desk. Reassured, I closed my eyes again, expecting to return to the scene, but it was gone. Now I could remember the scene, but it was different, just a memory. It was as if for a few seconds I had relived those long minutes after the accident, lying on the pavement beneath a June sky, waiting for help to arrive.

"OK, let's see how you are." Dr. Bell had me sit up, then walk across the room. She stayed close for the first few steps then watched me finish on my own.

"I'll see you in three weeks. Drink a lot of water." She emphasized the words *a lot.*

I gathered my things to leave and thanked her for the treatment. It seemed like some other part of me was looking out from behind my eyes, a part that had been away for a long time.

I saw Dr. Bell a few more times and each appointment was more remarkable than the one previous. On her table I relived a number of scenes from the accident. There was always a brief moment of fear as the tension of the cranial wave built inside me. Yet as soon as it released, I was filled with a great resting peace, a peace out of which sensory details from the accident emerged. I could see and smell, feel textures against my skin, but oddly there were neither sounds nor physical discomfort and never any emotional response to the treatment. Those came later. A few days or weeks following an osteopathy appointment, I would find myself unexpectedly full of feelings.

It was after my fourth appointment with Dr. Bell that the feelings finally became too big for me to hold. I was home one afternoon, catching up on some work, trying to write a response to a student's paper and laboring to name exactly what was wrong with it.

"God!" I said aloud, flinging the paper in frustration across my office, knocking a picture from the wall. Angrily, I got up from my desk and bent to pick up the picture. The glass in the frame had broken and spread in a web of spidery lines. Suddenly everywhere I looked, I saw spidery lines. It was as if the whole room was shattered. A sound began somewhere, a roaring sound like a train speeding through my head. I had no idea what was happening; whatever it was, it was terrifying.

I don't remember how I got from my office outside. The next thing I knew, I lay curled up on the gravel path in our garden crying. I don't know how long I lay there. When I finally stopped crying, I went to the phone and called a therapist for an appointment.

"I can't see you until next week," Renie said.

I had participated in a dream workshop that Renie facilitated some years earlier and from that experience, trusted both her counseling skills and her heart.

I rested my head against the wall by the phone, my eyes closed tightly. "No sooner?"

"No, I'm sorry."

Maybe if I had pressed Renie, told her what happened, how scared I felt that I might get lost again to the broken glass or the garden gravel, she would have found an earlier appointment for me. In fact, I feel certain that she would have, but I simply said I needed to see her.

"What's up?" she asked.

"I want to talk about an accident I had when I was 18."

Renie knew that I kept a journal and wrote poetry. "Can you write about it between now and when we meet?"

"I guess so." My voice sounded young, resigned, but I trusted Renie. After we hung up, I started writing: short pages, memory fragments, thoughts, the names of feelings—if I couldn't feel them, at least I could write their names. Over time, writing would become integral to my healing. Years later I would thank Renie for the start.

That is how I began seeing Renie Hope, a tall slender woman with autumn red hair, piercing blue eyes, and a flair for flowing and colorful clothing. As Dr. Bell's work opened me, Renie's helped me integrate what I discovered.

There was so much that I had not remembered. With Renie, I started placing the memories in some sort of sequence. Eventually, I could retrace the events of that June day in 1973 from their beginning to their end. I could hear the sound of glass breaking and metal shredding over pavement. I could recall the green slick wetness of the antifreeze as it ran from the overturned Jeep and puddled beneath me. I could hear the voices of my friends and remember the frantic things that they said. I remembered how chaotic the ride to the small town emergency room had been with one medic attending two patients, one requiring CPR. And finally, I could remember asking the emergency room doctor if my friend had died. I came to understand just how desperately I wanted his answer, an answer I could not bear to hear.

As I settled in upon Renie's couch, she prepared for our session by turning down the volume on her answering machine and closing her computer. Outside the daylight basement windows, it was spring, with forsythia in wild yellow bloom and white cherry blossoms sifting like spindrift on the slightest breeze. On the bookshelves beneath those windows were titles I knew well: *Group Therapy*, a classic by Irvin Yalom; *Extraordinary Relationships*, a newer primer on the family systems approach to counseling. Although I had not worked as a therapist, I had a master's degree in applied behavioral science and had trained to be one. I think I always knew that my own therapeutic work would have to come first. Instead, I became a teacher. Now I was finally motivated, out of necessity, to undertake the work.

Renie turned her chair to face me. "What is it that you want to talk about?"

"I want to talk about what happened last week."

"OK. Tell me."

I recounted everything, how frustrated I had become, the flinging of the paper, the spider lines, lying on the gravel path in our garden crying.

"You were really scared."

I nodded. On Renie's face I could see both care and concern in response to what I had said; the tenderness was enough to start me crying.

"Just let the feelings come."

Patiently, over time, Renie helped me to remember and more importantly, to feel what I could not feel at the time the events occurred. At first it seemed I did nothing but cry, but eventually I swore and hit at the pillows on the couch. The fury I felt at those who had left me holding the bag that day and the rest of my life was enormous. After one particular session of pillow pounding, as my breathing slowed, I felt a huge sadness descending over me.

"What's happening now, Cath?" Renie asked softly.

I shook my head, tears falling. "I don't hate any of them." Then in a quiet rush, "I miss them."

"You do miss them, you lost so much that day."

"I just want my mom to wrap me in her arms and make it all right again. I want that morning back; I want Rita back. I want my whole life back."

Renie stood up and reached for a throw that sat on the arm of her couch. Gently she laid it over my shoulders.

"No..." It was such a plaintive cry. I buried my face in my hands and wept.

Something changed in me that afternoon. I finally accepted not so much what happened, but that what had happened would never be fixed. I shifted, inside of me, the story of blame that I carried, blaming myself and blaming others, to a simpler story of loss: In the accident I had lost my innocence, my sense of belonging, my belief in my own goodness, my faith, and my hearing. Now I could finally grieve what had been lost rather than hold onto its pain. As I grieved the losses, I discovered the peace and gratitude hidden within their folds.

My sessions with Renie were never easy and there were times when I thought the depth of what I carried would drown me. It never did. Little by little, I could feel the progress I was making in a growing lightness of heart; I laughed more often and more heartily. Both my colleagues and my students started asking me if I had lost weight, or would say that I looked great.

Throughout 2001, I saw Renie once a week and Dr. Bell once a month. During my appointment in early November, Dr. Bell asked me about my hearing. I was sitting on her treatment table, putting my hearing aids back into my ears while waiting for her to finish writing in my chart.

"How is your hearing?" Dr. Bell asked, getting up and coming over to the table where I sat.

"OK, I guess."

"Have you noticed any changes?"

"I don't think so."

"Well," Dr. Bell paused, placing her hands on either side of my head and adjusting it ever so slightly. "You might notice some difference, a little here and there. Why don't you experiment between now and the next time I see you?"

All the way to the car, I wondered what she meant by a little here and a little there. Would I hear better, hear differently? I started listening extra hard, but nothing seemed different. Later that evening, while standing in the bedroom, I heard the phone ring in the kitchen. Hearing the phone ring was a hit-or-miss affair for me, so I decided that the house must be quieter than usual. Then when Dana and I crawled into bed, I took out my hearing aids as I always did. We shared some sweet words, kissed, and turned out the lights.

Lying there in the stillness, I thought about how I had almost always been able to hear Dana's voice speaking softly. That shouldn't have been possible. I thought about all the times when I had heard something in some situation that I normally would not. For instance: out walking, Dana would stop me and point out a hawk soaring overhead. She would ask me if I could hear its shrill whistle. Almost always I could not. Yet, there were times walking alone when that very same shrill whistle reached me and I would look up and see a hawk passing overhead. Dana shifted in bed beside me. Just before I slipped into dreams, I wondered: *How come there are times when I hear sounds that I shouldn't be able to hear? What is that about?*

Gradually, I started hearing more sounds. Maybe I was just listening harder, paying more attention, but the truth was undeniable. I started leaving my hearing aids out for longer periods of time. The change was subtle, but definitely there.

Dana was the only person I told, because I could hardly believe what was happening. I had worn hearing aids for 20 years. It was part of my identity: I was hard of hearing. All of a sudden, hearing was getting easier and after Dana, Dr. Bell was the person I was most eager to tell. At my next appointment, I did not wait for Dr. Bell to ask the question: How are you? Instead I started right in the moment she entered the room.

"You were right, I am hearing better, I mean really better."

She smiled and nodded her head slightly. "What seems different?"

"I hear the phone ring, I hear when Dana is talking with someone in another part of the house. I hear birds singing—not always, but I hear them."

"You've come a long way." Dr. Bell's eyes softened. "Sometimes miracles really happen." Then she placed her hand on the treatment table. "Let's have you up."

That session was like most of the others, except at the very end. Dr. Bell cradled my head in her hands gently. The whole room seemed to still and I settled into a deep, expansive, and spacious silence. For me time stopped, thoughts stopped. Somewhere in that peace, I became aware of a presence; and then of that presence—departing. Dr. Bell slowly drew her hands from my head. As she slid them away, I could feel her going too. Not only had Dr. Bell's hands held my body, once a month for the last nine, she had held my heart's healing as well.

Quietly she left the treatment room, the door closing softly behind her. I knew then that this appointment would be my last. Dr. Bell had said goodbye without words, and although I cannot explain it, I know I felt it. At the front desk as I was writing my check, she did indeed declare our work finished, wished me well, and sent me on my way.

My hearing loss had been psychosomatic—it was a very real defense against the world, a way to buffer myself from its pain and my own. In finally facing my grief, I discovered a greater gratitude for living. That well of gratitude gave me the necessary compassion and courage to meet the world without hiding. On December 15, 2001, at the age of 46, I removed my hearing aids for the last time and have never worn them again.

US Highway 50

Of all the highways and back roads that I have driven and cycled in this country, US Highway 50 is my favorite—especially the stretch that runs across central Nevada. Dubbed on truck-stop T-shirts as the "Loneliest Road in America," it traverses a land inhabited by few; it crosses a country where the same geologic theme repeats itself, over and over, an accordant landscape of dry mountain ranges and broad desert basins. What towns remain survive by providing services to travelers and supplies to the handful of ranchers and miners who still scrape a living from the land. The last time I drove this stretch of road, I remembered how important it is to look again, to respect myself and others, to stay in touch with what is true.

Winding down from an 8,000-foot pass through hairpin after hairpin turn, the smell of hot rubber settled across the back seat like an unwelcome hitchhiker. In my rearview mirror, I watched the state of Utah and the faces of my loved ones fall further behind. I had just left Alex at boarding school in Colorado and Dana at the airport in Salt Lake City. As a result, I was now on my own: a middle-aged woman, temporarily freed of her responsibilities—with the entire state of Nevada, 1000 miles of road, and 5 solitary days ahead. The sudden freedom was intoxicating. I belted out my entire repertoire of known songs through that series of turns. Just when I was about to start over, the grade eased, the road straightened, and the vast Great Basin desert opened before me.

Lowering the windows in the car, I sniffed the early morning air like a coyote in search of a scent. My life moves too quickly these days. I mistake the urgent for the important and get overextended in too many directions. Over time, like the thin and rangy dogs of the desert, I too grow hungry, hungry for silence and solitude. The open road offers both. Since the day I got my driver's license, so many years ago, and in spite of my accident, when I have needed time alone—I have gotten in a car and driven there.

I come to my love of driving honestly. While other dads worked in offices, mine worked behind the wheel, spending Monday through Friday driving from one manufacturing plant to another, crisscrossing the industrial Midwest in his Cadillac convertible. Every once in a while he took me along.

In my memory, those trips are always on bright, autumn days. Mom waves goodbye to us at the door, and soon we are out of the city and traveling through farmland. We ride with the top down, even if it is cold. Dad simply turns up the heat and blasts the fan. We drink Coca-Cola, play the radio loud, and sing songs. The Notre Dame fight song is our favorite. In the midafternoon when the road appears empty, Dad lets me slide across the big leather bench seat and climb into his lap. He places my 7-year-old hands on the wheel with his larger ones next to them. Wrapped in his confident arms and Old Spice aftershave, I truly believe that I am driving.

A red-tailed hawk glides low over the brown earth, crosses in front of me, and hunts the land to my left. It has been over an hour since I saw another car, 3 hours since I left my campsite. Like an airline passenger bored with her book, I strike up a casual conversation with my red-tailed companion. I tell hawk about my life, about the things that worry me. Hawk listens well, showing neither too much interest, nor too much boredom.

"I am tired of juggling all the plates," I say. "Work, friends, family, writing…" I sigh, feeling the pull of so many responsibilities and commitments.

Rarely am I able to engage as fully as I would like to any one of them. The answer seems obvious. Let go of one, but which? Each seems so important. With strong wing beats, my companion circles up and back, leaving me with my questions. I wish for hawk's keen eye and long view. What is it like, I wonder, to be a dark shape flying before the sun, to spread wingtips like fingers and read the wind like a map of Braille? I envy the hawk's ability to follow his instinct; I too often follow the rules.

One of the rules I follow is to be patient with a world that is routinely blind to my partnership with another woman. I considered the social gymnastics we recently performed at Alex's school.

"Which one is your child?" an interested parent asked, as Dana and I stood together in the cafeteria line.

Dana pointed across the crowded dining room at the smiling boy, who is taller than both of us, and quickly becoming a man, and said, "Alex."

Then the interested parent turned to me.

"And you? Do you have a son or daughter here?"

"Yes," I replied, pointing at the same young man, "Alex."

The confused look and alternating glances from one of our proud faces to the other gave away the inquirer's surprise and slow recognition that we were a lesbian couple. It would be so refreshing in those moments to hear some admission of the other's surprise, some recognition of our difference. Instead, most are quick to cover their feelings, and even quicker to minimize the difference by saying something like, "Oh, hey that's great," or "Wow. Well, don't you think the food here is pretty good?" I long for recognition of our difference. Such recognition is the first step in discovering how much we are alike.

Ready for a stretch break, I leave the pavement and follow a dirt track to a rocky outcrop. After a few bone-jarring minutes of impossible road, I am sitting in the shaded silence of a limestone tower, sipping the last of the morning's coffee. My stainless-steel thermos lies next to me like a shiny artifact jettisoned from the future. Everything else here feels old: weathered stone breaks off and crumbles in my hand, bits of bone and pieces of rusted metal can be found lying everywhere, even the wind seems to speak in an ancient whisper. From where I sit, I can see the highway below, lying like a dark ribbon across a pale brown package. A car approaches and passes, moves like a toy and shines like a bauble. But it too is quickly gone, its flash disappearing in the distance.

The world I know is changing. For the first time in 10 years, Dana and I will be living without children at home. At the same time, my mother and father are showing signs of their aging: my father can no longer travel and my mother forgets the things she has told me. My place of work has recently relocated and I have been promoted. On top of all this, or perhaps because of all this, I have been feeling tired and restless. Friends reassure me that my feelings are not atypical for a woman in her mid-forties. But knowing that I am not unusual among my gender or my age group does little to relieve the low-level anxiety I feel. In the few quiet moments that I am able to carve out each day, I find myself increasingly asking for direction, watching for signs, searching for something that will help me through this time of change and uncertainty. In some ways the answers were already revealing themselves on this trip: take more time, follow my instincts, stop when I need a break.

A little further down the road a couple of Airstream trailers, each with a collection of rusted cars and broken appliances cluttering their dusty yards, announce that I am approaching civilization. Beyond these stand worn-looking houses with faded and peeling paint, an abandoned church with windows and door boarded over. I am driving into the historic town of Eureka, Nevada.

Once a thriving mining town—many of whose wooden storefronts and boardwalks remain—the place today looks more like a western movie set in the midst of either going up, or coming down. Some buildings are in the process of being restored while others warp and buckle into further disrepair. Overall, there is a sense of time running out here, of people running out—out of cash, out of good reasons and the will to live in such a place. Those who do carry on, do so with necessary resolve, accepting the inevitable hardship of life and eventual loss of neighbors. Shopkeepers act friendly, but also guarded. They do not hurry to help me and seem comfortable with my aimless browsing; most continue to do whatever it was that they were doing when I came in, banging the little bells that hang above their doors. And yet whenever I looked, I found them watching me. Were they curious, suspicious, maybe both?

Looking back, I think I was just lonely that afternoon. The brief responses that seemed indifferent to my questions, the watchfulness that seemed somehow suspicious simply added weight, a couple more stones to a heavy pack of memories, musings, and considerations. I decided to move on. Before leaving town, I pulled into a whitewashed building with a set of gas pumps in front. I needed a bathroom and the car needed gas.

The E-Z Stop Café was a multi-purpose establishment, operating as a mini-mart, liquor store, gas station, short-order restaurant, and pool hall. Stepping inside, out of the harsh desert light, my eyes opened wide, trying to get my bearings and discern the details of the dimly lit interior. A loud crack startled me, banging my heart inside my chest even as I recognized the sound—a cue ball breaking against a tightly racked set. Against the far wall, three Native men seemed to be more or less engaged in a game of pool. On the near side of the room, two middle-aged white women worked behind a lunch counter. One handled the fry baskets and grill, while the other was making a milkshake. When I asked if there was a restroom I could use, the milkshake woman nodded. With her left hand she kept the metal cup pressed beneath the blender's spindle, while with her right, she reached for a smoldering cigarette. After a deep inhale, she used it as a pointer, extending her arm in the direction of the pool table and what appeared to be a large plywood box jutting from the wall behind it. In the middle of the box stood a door with a tin sign nailed above it. The sign read "Ladies." And, just below the sign, leaning against the door with an expressionless face, arms crossed over an enormous chest, legs spread slightly apart, stood a very big man.

I am not a small or generally fearful woman, but my legs felt weak. The pool game had stopped and all dark eyes were focused on me. Like figures in a modern-day diorama, we faced each other. I could have stepped off the pages of an outdoor travel magazine: white, middle-aged, professional woman with short hair, wearing baggy shorts, flip-flops, a rumpled white cotton shirt with the sleeves rolled up and the tails un-tucked. Around my neck, on a colorful strap hung an expensive pair of sunglasses. Across the room, separated by a few steps and a pool table with worn green felt, stood three young Shoshone warriors. Each was dressed in "gangsta" black, trademarked by Nike, Massimo, and Gap. Each appeared as tall or taller than me, built larger and square. Like boxes made of stone, they leaned on their pool cues and stared. From beneath their baseball caps turned backwards, hair the color of obsidian hung loose and long.

As a woman traveling alone, I am aware that the line between adventure and danger can be thin. Standing there in that rural Nevada café, I could feel my fear leaking into the stillness. Cold seeped into my limbs while sweat ran from beneath my arms. I weighed the awful possibilities against the more likely probabilities. Meanwhile, the women behind the counter kept busy, either oblivious or unconcerned about what was developing. Maybe it was because nothing was developing. Taking a deep breath, I walked across the room and stopped in front of the ladies room door. The young man who had been leaning against it had not moved. I avoided meeting his eyes. He smelled strong: musty with a hint of tobacco and a fruity scent, like chewing gum. Raising my hand ever so slightly, I made a feeble pointing gesture to the sign above the door. Seconds passed like minutes. Who was I to him? What did he see: whiteness, a woman alone, a lesbian? I turned the question back to me: Who did I see? The answer was easy: an angry Indian, a dangerous man. The surety of my response stunned me. I teach college courses in diversity and know better. I could be sure of only what I had seen: gender, skin color, clothing, and stance; the rest I had interpreted, filled in, and made up. I took another deep breath; this time I looked directly at him and said:

"Excuse me, I'd like to use the bathroom."

Another excruciatingly long second passed. Then, the young man stepped aside. Gratefully, I went in and locked the door. As I sat down on the toilet seat, my heart pounded with relief. My pee sounded like a waterfall pouring into the quiet. It was the expressionless, unflinching way they had watched me that had frightened me, but did they intend to frighten me? Lacking real information about their motives, I had filled in the blanks with fear. I have no personal history that explains the level of fear that I felt. In fact what I experienced felt larger than me, larger and very old. It was as if, in that moment, I had carried all the fear of everyone who has grown up a girl in this country.

I washed my hands and my face, and then looked into a shard of mirror that hung on the wall. I hate it when people do not see me, but instead see only what they fear or do not understand. I knew absolutely nothing about those three young men outside, nothing about the quality of their hearts.

When I opened the ladies room door and stepped out, it was as if time had stood still. No one had moved; apparently, not even a muscle. But if they had not changed, I had. I no longer felt afraid. Instead, I was determined. I looked at every single one of the young men, nodded and smiled. I looked at the shot still waiting on the table. "Think you can sink it?" I asked the one who had earlier blocked my way. The hint of a smile played at the corners of his mouth. "Nine ball, corner pocket?" I called the shot I saw, albeit tentatively. He tipped his cue stick as if in agreement. I felt my shoulders relax and I smiled again. As I stepped out into the midday glare, I heard the crack of a cue ball behind me, followed by the thud of a ball finding its pocket.

Small towns are like people: they have good days and bad days—visits when they seem friendly, visits when they seem cold. Driving out of town, I thought about returning to Eureka. Maybe I will explore a little more, talk to people, feel brave enough to shoot a game of pool. I also thought about how difficult it is to admit fear or surprise when those feelings are so obviously present. As I drove, I began to see the parents who I met at Alex's boarding school with softer eyes. They had done the best they could, in the moment, with Dana and me as well.

The rest of the afternoon, I watched as thunderheads built over distant mountains and the morning's blue sky retreated before an advancing mass of gray. Occasionally, a shaft of sunlight pierced the growing darkness, illuminating the land with what one friend calls "religious light." As I drove closer to the approaching weather, I felt lighter in my heart. The wind riding in through the open windows felt moist and cool. I was content. Glancing at the speedometer, I saw that I was traveling at 70 mph, yet I had no sense that I was traveling fast. It seemed that I had the road completely to myself, a road extending straight ahead for as far as the eye could see. If I only had this moment and no others after it, how would I live? I slipped a CD into the player and turned the volume up as far as it would go. I knew the track I wanted, Shawn Colvin's "Shotgun Down The Avalanche." As the bass beat poured through the speakers, it filled my body, opening me wide. Electric guitar riffs whined through my skull and wired me tight. For a few seconds the tension held, like a "mountain of new fallen snow." I drove the gas pedal to the floor. The car shuddered, then shot forward as pistons pumped and valves gaped. I too felt made of fluid and fire.

At 80, 90, 110 mph, the wind bellowed through the open windows and drowned the music. I felt as large and full as the land over which I was hurtling. Visions of cascading waterfalls tumbling down cliffs, wild marshes thick with the flushing of birds, seas of prairie grass rolling towards the horizon, meandering rivers heavy with fish—all flashed in my mind, filling the barren landscape around me with life.

Suddenly, as if my heart had called them, a herd of pronghorn antelope—some twenty or thirty animals—were running full speed beside me. I lifted my foot from the accelerator, slipped the car out of gear, switched off the engine. For a few glorious seconds, I was sailing silently down the empty highway. The wind lessened. The sounds of the herd grew louder: hooves glancing off hard stones, like flint against steel. It was as if I could hear coarse and heavy breathing, the effort of muscles, small throaty cries rising over the rhythm of the run. Then, as quickly as they had appeared, they veered away. The car coasted to a stop. The air smelled sweet and everything was still.

What comes to us is a gift. There is a Buddhist Sutra that states:

And all that is mine, beloved and pleasing,
will become otherwise,
and will one day become separated from me.

I am the owner of my actions,
heir to my actions, born of my actions,
related to my actions,
abided and supported by my actions.
Whatever action I shall do,
for good or for ill, of that I will be the heir.

My entire life, all of it, is a gift, a fleeting and beautiful gift. Even the accident, although tragic, has made me who I am; by grace I have been given life.

Mom

Like the deer who thirsts for running water,
so my soul thirsts for God.
Psalm 42

In November of 2006, my mother passed away after a 2-year walk with cancer as her constant companion. Dana and I traveled to Indianapolis to spend the last 3 weeks of her life with her. My father had cared for her at home until he was no longer able. She spent her last weeks in a beautiful hospice facility on the north side of the city.

St. Vincent's Hospice was bordered on one side by fields and woodlands and on the other, by a residential street. At the edge of the city, it was a sanctuary of peace and quiet. Every room had a small living area that opened into a bedroom, a set of French doors that looked out upon a garden filled with flowering shrubs, winding pathways, and roses everywhere. A small pond in the garden's center provided the soothing sound of falling water. It was there that we kept my mother's vigil; there, that I thought back to her seventy-second birthday earlier in the spring.

"Mom, what made you happy?" I had asked her one morning on that spring visit. She was still living at home then, wrapped in a silk robe, reclining on a chaise that was set beside an east-facing window. The sun shown behind her, it was morning, a new day, and it was spring. Dana and I had come for her birthday; we all thought it would be her last. Her cancer had returned, metastasized, and spread aggressively to her spine, brain, and liver. She declined another round of chemotherapy, preferring to have a few months without the nausea, weakness, and fatigue that she felt when receiving it.

"I am most happy," she said, "when I can help you or Dad with something you are working on."

That was my mother and in many ways me too, someone who could feel happy being of service to others. "I know Mom, but what made you happy… before Dad and me?" I pressed her gently, wanting something I could hold onto, that would convince me that I had really known her. She was such a private person, rarely sharing her own thoughts or feelings unless asked directly.

"Well, when I was a girl, when we lived on Meridian Street—"

I knew the house to which she was referring and nodded.

"—I would come home after school and go upstairs…" she closed her eyes for a minute remembering, or just tired, I was not sure. "I would go upstairs and sit in that window seat; remember it?"

"The one outside the boys' bedrooms?"

She nodded her head, perhaps picturing her younger brothers.

"I would curl up with my favorite book of the moment and read. If the sun were out, it was all the better. It would be so warm there, I would fall asleep, the best sleep."

The thought of a younger her drifting into a sun-warmed nap touched my heart. "Mamma, I love you."

"I love you too, honey." We both started to cry. "But I know that you will be OK."

"I will," I said, wiping my tears with my sleeve.

"It's your dad; I don't know how he will manage."

"He'll be OK too." I wanted to reassure her although I harbored the same thought. I knew even then how hard she had fought to keep up the appearance of health all these months when she had been so very sick. She did it to protect my father. It was a long habit employed by both of us.

Later that same morning, I came back in from the kitchen and found my mother asleep in her chaise, the sun pouring in through that east-facing window, a book open on her lap. I stood there for some time, tears running down my cheeks. The picture was just like her story; she must have been truly happy.

My mother's birthday fell on a Friday. My father had business to attend to south of the city; otherwise he would have been with us. Instead it was Mom, Dana, and me—a day with just us girls. Mom awoke feeling excited, possessing an energy she had not had for a very long time. She dressed herself in a lightweight gray suit and pink silk blouse. She slipped on a pair of fashionable heels, and adorned herself with a few pieces of her favorite jewelry. She was ready to go when we came for her. Dad had requested a Mass be said for my mother and had instructed Dana and me to take her to church and then out to a birthday lunch. One of the ways I knew that my mother was much sicker than she let on was that she had stopped going to Mass. All her life, my mother attended daily Mass. Over the last year though, she had rarely attended. But today, she was going no matter what.

Mom needed assistance to walk from the house to the car. Dana offered her elbow and I walked ahead. Mom loved Dana. She felt something special for her, I think because they both had lost their own mothers early in life. Dana's mother passed away just after Alex was born, when Dana was 32. My mother was only 12 when hers died, but I think, in my mother's mind, it gave them something in common. Mom was also genuinely curious about Dana's thinking on things. Once when my father was trying to control the conversation at the dinner table, Dana had stood up to him, gently but firmly. I will never forget the look on my mother's face; she was at first surprised and then obviously proud of Dana's strength and character. How much had she held herself from saying all these years?

St. John's Cathedral is one of the oldest churches in Indianapolis. Dark and gothic with frescos of angels adorning the high domed ceiling, it is a cavernous place full of quiet alcoves, flickering votives, and dancing shadows. Mom and Dad had adopted it as their parish precisely because it was elegant and an old-fashioned church. Every Sunday there was one Mass that was still said in Latin.

I escorted Mom down the aisle. There were a handful of elderly parishioners scattered about, otherwise the church stood virtually empty. Mom stopped about halfway down, indicating she'd like us to kneel here.

"Mom, it's a pretty long walk down for communion," I whispered.

"Father Noah will bring it." She patted my hand with hers.

To be together there clearly made her glad and it did me too. Sitting beside her, I could feel the calm settle upon her entire being the minute the ritual began. On that day I also heard how labored her breathing had become.

I do not recall much about the Mass itself that day. I do remember that it meant the world to sit close to my mother, sometimes holding her hand, helping her to her feet when it was time to stand. Touching her seemed vital. It was as if I was remembering me to her and her to me, so that when she died I would still be able to feel her with my skin and my body, how she had been enfolded in my hugs, how she had wobbled beside me on bad hips and circulation-starved feet. I did not actually think about these things; it has only been with the passage of time that I see all the nuances of that simple event, of attending Mass with my mother on her birthday. The next time I would attend Mass at St. John's would be for her funeral. But on that May morning, I simply enjoyed being at my mother's side. I could not have been happier: to have the two women who had taught me the most about love—together, my mother and my partner—felt so very sweet.

After Mass, the three of us climbed into the car and considered our lunch options. "Do you want to go to the Museum for lunch?" I asked, knowing my mother liked the restaurant at the Indianapolis Museum of Art.

"It's your birthday, Cay," Dana said from the back seat. "Where do you want to have lunch?"

"I want to have a picnic."

"A picnic?" I felt surprised by my mother's response. Here was a woman who wore heels the way the rest of us wear house slippers, whose suits were some of the best that money could buy. "You want to have a picnic?"

"Yes, we can go to that deli at 52nd and College. They have really good sandwiches and little salads and desserts."

The way she said *desserts,* as if referring to a guilty pleasure, I knew she was looking forward to that part of lunch most of all.

"Where will we eat our picnic?" I asked carefully, hoping it wouldn't be in the car. She and my father often reported to me that they had had a lovely *picnic,* sitting in their car parked beside a liquor store or burned-out warehouse. It was not my idea of a birthday luncheon. *But it's her birthday.*

"So, Mom, where shall we picnic?"

My mother thought, then she said: "I know." Her face had a slightly mischievous look to it. "Holcomb Gardens, by the waterfall."

"OK," Dana and I said in unison, both relieved we'd be eating outside rather than in the car.

Loaded with roast beef sandwiches, each with a healthy dollop of horseradish, dill pickle spears, small sacks of potato chips, three cold beers, and a strawberry tart to share, we were off to Butler University and Holcomb Gardens. The house I grew up in was a block from the University and although Dana had seen it before, I drove us by. Mom tapped her long nails against the glass.

"Look how they let that side patio go."

The brick wall had fallen, its bricks scattered about what used to be a quiet little grotto where we kept an iron bench and a statue of the Blessed Mother. Mom shook her head. "The rest of the place doesn't look too bad." She emphasized the word *too* as if reassuring herself.

When we arrived at the gardens, I pulled the car up as close to the waterfall as I could. Dana and I helped Mom out and then Dana walked her across the grass to a park bench. I remember being so touched by Dana's strength and sureness guiding Mom, who tottered in her stiletto heels across the rich green grass. A friend who has a beautiful garden once recalled my parents' visit by saying: "And Cay, in those heels, she aerated the lawn..." I smiled as I watched the two of them now, heading for the bench: my mother aerating the way. We had our picnic lunch. Mom ate half her sandwich and almost all of the dessert, and as we drove back to their condominium, I could tell she was very weak, but happy and content.

My mother did indeed have the summer she imagined when she declined further chemotherapy. Still living in her home, she regained enough energy to do all the things she and my father loved to do together. They sat outside in lawn chairs and read the *New York Times*. They played chess and gin rummy, they attended daily Mass once again, and picnicked often in Dad's Jaguar parked in the dirtiest and roughest of places, dressed to the nines, oblivious to the world.

On the 29th of September that year, my mother collapsed. Dad called and told me.

"What can we do?" he asked.

"There's nothing we can do, Dad. We just have to be with her."

"I can't go to that place." My father was referring to the hospice facility where Mom had been taken and would remain. Dad's fear of hospitals was well known to both Mom and me. The idea of the hospice facility scared him even more.

"You can do it, Dad."

"Umph," was all he said before hanging up.

I flew to Indianapolis and saw my mother settled into her room at St. Vincent's Hospice. She had grown so thin and frail in the last few weeks; I couldn't believe she was the same woman with whom I had shared a garden bench just 4 months earlier.

"Hi Mom," I said, as she opened her eyes.

"Hum?"

I pulled my chair close to the side of the bed. "Did you have a good rest?"

"Was I sleeping?"

"Uh-huh."

"Oh." She seemed a little surprised.

"Mom," I began and then faltered. It was so important to me that we name what was happening. "Mom, you know you are dying."

"I know, honey."

I couldn't stop. "I will miss you so much. I love talking to you, every day!" We were both crying. "I will still call you whether you are in Indianapolis or in heaven."

"The phone bill might get expensive," she said softly.

We laughed a little through our tears.

"I'll put the call in every morning when I pray."

Her voice grew serious. "I hope I go quickly. I don't want you and Dad to go through a lot of pain."

"I don't want you to suffer."

She paused, then reached for my hand. "You know when I get to heaven, I'll be able to help you and Dad, and Dana and Kate and Alex, so much more than I can here. It'll take me a while, but I will learn how it's done." She squeezed my hand.

If the dead can intercede in the lives of the living, I know my mother will be hard at work on the other side. "I know you Mom, you will figure it out."

My mother closed her eyes, then softly said: "You'll be OK, you're strong."

That was the last conversation she and I would have. She could and did rouse herself to consciousness when people with whom she needed to say more came to her bedside, but when she had said her goodbye, in whatever way, she would no longer wake for that person when they returned.

It was almost Halloween and we had been anticipating Mom's death for almost 3 weeks. We sat with her daily: Dana quilting, me journaling or reading, both of us hosting the friends and family who came to visit. At night Dana would go to our friends' house to sleep and I would pull out the sofa bed in the sitting area; I did not want to leave my mother's side.

One afternoon her friend and the Pastor of St. John's Cathedral, Father Noah, came and visited. She did not open her eyes for him, but smiled when he greeted her. Dana and I stood a little apart from them as Father prayed for her. Slowly the room seemed to brighten even though it was late afternoon and quite foggy outside. Mom began to smile and the room started to glow, as if someone had lit a hundred candles. Dana and I kept exchanging glances as if to confirm that what we were witnessing was truly happening. We could feel a growing presence among us, one that I can only name as love. The room was bathed in light, the expansiveness of love was among us, and Mom was at peace. I remember thinking *this is it, she will stop breathing now*, but she did not. She continued in the same erratic pattern that had become all too familiar: a breath then a long pause, an unnaturally long pause, then a gasping inhale.

Father Noah blessed my mother one more time. "Our Lord has big plans for you, Mary Cay." My mother smiled once more.

Dana and I walked Father Noah to his car and thanked him for coming. It was almost dusk as we stood outside in the cold and watched him drive away. "Look!" Dana said. I thought she might have seen a glimpse of the moon, which had been showing itself getting fuller as the week progressed.

"Where?"

"There. Look." She pointed to the street that ran in front of the facility. A very large buck was bounding down it, heading right for the busy boulevard. Even in the dim light, we could see he was an enormous animal with a huge antler rack. Just then he disappeared into a subdivision across the street. The sight of it took our breath away. Later we agreed that it was a sign, although we still could not quite believe what we had seen. The next day's newspaper reassured us, front-page news that read something like *Large stag sighted on city's north side*; apparently we were not the only ones who had seen the deer.

Mom lived another week. My father, who had stayed away from the hospice, finally came to her. He knelt beside her bed, took her hand, and kissed it.

"Korea was easy," he said, meaning the war. "This is so much harder." He was clear and calm, different than I had seen him since we had arrived. The three of us sat by Mom's bed, talking quietly. On the little altar that Dana had constructed, votives flickered and violin music played ever so softly from the CD player.

Seemingly out of the blue, my father turned to me and asked: "Would you show me around?"

"Sure, let's go." He and I walked, holding hands, down to the family room. A Notre Dame game was playing on the big screen TV. We watched for a minute or two. We walked to the sunroom that looked out upon the garden.

"This is really nice," he said, as if seeing the place for the first time.

In many ways this was the first time, the first time he had been truly present with my mother, with Dana, and with me since Mom's collapse. We returned to my mother's room and he kissed her good-bye. Dana and I slipped out into the hall to give them some privacy together. We could not overhear what he said, but we could hear the soft lament in his voice. When he was finished visiting her, we helped him with his coat. Then, when he was ready, we walked him to his car, which he had left outside the front door.

"It's good that I came," he said, half statement, half question.

"Yes, Dad, it is; it's good for both of you."

"Call me if anything changes."

"I will."

Dana and I went back to Mom's room. I went over to sit beside her, Dana stood next to me. My mother breathed, nothing more than a sip of air and then… then she was gone. I looked at Dana: "Is she…?"

"I think so."

We waited, looking with quiet awe at her face so completely relaxed, mouth slightly open. After a minute or so it was clear that she was dead. I felt something move and turned to look at the French doors. Nothing was there. No, I thought, she was there, just for a moment, her soul's last look before slipping out into the forever night.

As if on cue, Robin, the evening shift nurse, came in to check Mom's vitals.

"I think she's gone," I said, looking up and clearing my throat.

Robin looked at my mother, then at Dana and me. A slight smile crossed her face and there was deep caring in her eyes. She knew all of us were free now from the long wait.

"What time?"

"5:20," Dana and I said in unison.

She wrote it down, said something kind, hugged us both, and left the room.

Dana put her arms around me. "Oh, sweetheart."

"She is really gone, isn't she?"

"Yes, she is."

I rested against my love for a moment, then wiped the tears from my eyes and called my dad, knowing he was not very far away.

"Mom's gone, Dad. Mom's in heaven."

"How do you know?"

"She stopped breathing."

"Oh. OK, I'll be right there."

It all happened in a matter of minutes. My dad returned, kissed his wife, his companion of 50 years, one last time.

"You say your goodbyes," he instructed me. "Call me after Matt comes." Then my father went home. I don't know what he did that night or how he passed the time. I hope he too was relieved that the waiting was finally over and that Mom was now freed from her suffering.

I called Matt the undertaker and asked him to come for Mom after 9:00 PM. Then I called those who had been closest to Mom in her last days. The woman who had done my mother's nails for 20 years showed up first, and together with Dana and me, we washed my mother's body. Tears ran down my face as I touched my mother's long slender arms, her soft cheek, the hollow behind her knees. This was my mother who gave me life, who loved me unconditionally. How do I say goodbye?

We dressed my mother in yellow silk pajamas, brushed her hair, and folded her hands on top of the covers that we had straightened. Our friends arrived, bringing a pot of sweet potato soup. Someone uncorked a bottle of champagne and we toasted my mother, her good life, and our good fortune to be together at this moment. Those present were Dick and Peg, my mother and father's oldest friends. Dick had been my father's best man and Peg, my mother's maid of honor. Carolyn and her partner Prov; Carolyn had gone through grade school with my mother and been my fourth grade teacher. Over the last couple of years, Dana and I had become very close with the two of them, and stayed with them whenever we were in town. Dawneil also came. For over a decade, she had helped my mother with bookkeeping and taxes. My mother often referred to Dawneil as her other daughter. The seven of us toasted Mom, saying our last goodbyes, crying with each other and laughing too; I knew my mother would be so pleased. Eventually, everyone left and the undertaker arrived. I kissed my mother one more time and then let her go.

Dana and I gathered up the last of Mom's things as well as a few of our own, blew out the candles, and left what had become a second home for us over the last month. As we walked out into the parking lot, we could see the moon moving in and out behind the clouds. It was a very cold November night, frost forming on the ground. We had just closed the trunk of the car when Dana reached for my arm.

"Oh my God!"

"What?" Then I saw it too. The Stag. This time he was running on the woodland side of the hospice, running the opposite direction, running through the open field to the forest, running home.

My mother's whole life was one long conversation with God. She was a devout Catholic, a daily communicant but most importantly, a woman of faith. My mother believed not only in God, but also in

God's immeasurable love for the world. Prayers were her way of expressing thanks for that love, of finding solace and comfort in it as well. She, with all her heart, hoped that I would discover the same gratitude and refuge, the same peace, one larger and more complete than any other on earth. This was my mother's greatest prayer. And, it is one that God has truly answered.

EPILOGUE

In 2015, for my sixtieth birthday, Dana and I walked the Camino de Santiago Compostela: an ancient Christian pilgrimage route that stretches 500 miles across the north of Spain. When people asked why I wanted to do such a thing, I would reply: "I want to make a really big prayer, to give thanks for my life." My answer often sounded embarrassingly simple, but it was the truth. I am grateful for my life.

Dana and I are legally married, an opportunity I never dreamed would be possible. Together, we grow food on 2 acres of beautiful land. After 18 years of academic life, I traded in my syllabi for a shovel and a hoe. It's not a typical midlife choice but one that continues to nourish me (as well as a few other people) every day. Kate and Alex are now well into their thirties, living full and rich lives, both doing what they love. I cannot imagine my life without them. My dad is dead, buried next to my mother in a small cemetery north of Indianapolis. It was a holy privilege to accompany both my mother and my father to their final gate. In the last weeks, days, hours, and minutes of their lives I felt our history, as well as our future, compress into each cycle of breath; as the pauses between inhalations and exhalations grew, it was only love and kindness that made any sense. And somewhere along the way, I returned to the practice of my Catholic faith. Making peace with the failures of the church seemed to go hand in hand with making peace with me. The gospel of Christ, as a way of living, inspires me deeply. The decision to walk the Camino was a way to reflect on all of this, reflect and give thanks.

There were so many stories, small miracles, and amazing moments on that walk across Spain, but this is the one that has stayed with me the most.

Dana and I had been walking for over a week. It was midmorning in some small village whose name I can't remember. We crossed through a cobblestone square where we saw a young woman sitting on a stone wall outside a church. We had seen her earlier in the trip walking with a band of other young pilgrims. They were a boisterous and big-spirited group. But on this particular morning, she was alone.

"Buen Camino," we said in greeting.

"Buen Camino," she replied. The saying is as much a hello as it is a goodbye. It can be said with the lightest of intention and with the deepest respect, shouted heartily and whispered softly. *Buen Camino—May your way go well.*

"Michelle? Is it Michelle?" I thought I remembered her name.

"Yes? Hi. I'm sorry; what's your name?"

"Catherine."

She nodded.

"Did you go to Mass?" I pointed at the church door where the Mass times were posted. There had been one earlier that morning.

"No, but it is a beautiful church... so simple."

"I know; the big cathedrals don't move me near as much as these small village churches."

"They're humble," she said firmly, as if stating a fact.

"I'm not going to be able to finish," she continued, "my ankle is bad." She pointed down to a very swollen right ankle wrapped in tape.

Earlier, Dana and I had noticed her limping and thought maybe she was carrying too much; her pack was twice the size of the ones we carried.

"Are you sure? Couldn't you take some days off and rest it?"

She looked into the distance. Santiago was still weeks away.

"I'm sure," she said, still looking towards her goal.

"What are you going to do?"

She turned and looked down at her ankle. "I'll walk a little each day, even if it's only a few steps, and then… I'll go home."

"I'm so sorry." I could only imagine my own disappointment if I was unable to go on.

"I'm not," she said, now looking directly at me. "God has me, right where he wants me."

Even though we left Michelle behind, her statement walked with me for the rest of the trip and has stayed with me since. I have turned it over in my mind a thousand times. I have come to believe that this is what she meant.

God, by whatever name we call her, by whatever pronoun we assign him, by whatever way we experience it, does not make us suffer. Our humanness makes us suffer. Our humanness causes others to suffer. But our humanness can also open us to something greater, to God's love and mercy. When we are suffering, broken, disappointed, or lost—we are sitting on that stone wall, watching our future, the one we carefully planned, dissolve before our eyes. But God is right there, sitting next to us if we only can hear its whisper, turn, and see his many faces, recognize her grace.

For years, my guilt and my regret, my stubborn belief that I, alone, had to figure everything out, make everything right, kept me from seeing God's presence beside me. During those years, I was sustained by the beauty of the natural world, but is that not God? Dana's love opened my heart. Is that not God as well? Teachers and healers appeared to help me find my way. Is that not also God? Feeling called to love and serve my family, friends, and community; that too is God, sitting next to me.

Just before we left for Spain, a prayer came to me. I did not compose it but just discovered myself saying it. On the Camino, I said it every morning upon waking and every night before sleep and several times a day as we walked those many miles. It is the way I would like to live the rest of my life.

I am walking praising you oh God.
I am walking for the healing of the earth,
for an end to nuclear power and weapons,
for all beings everywhere that they may be free of suffering.
I am walking with gratitude for my family and friends,
with gratitude for the ancestors and for those yet to be born
that theirs will be a more peaceful, just, and verdant world.
I am walking in wonder of the great mystery,
May each step I take be with humility, courage, and compassion.
I am walking praising you oh God.
I am walking.

We all are.

Buen Camino.

ACKNOWLEDGMENTS

I wish to thank Brenda Peterson who convinced me that I had a story to tell and then spent 10 years patiently teaching me the craft. This book would not exist were it not for you. And, to all the women of Brenda's Monday evening writing class who read my first tentative scenes, your critique was always balanced with tender caring; thank you. Especially, thank you to Laura Foreman for your colleagueship and ideal editing. You believed in the book, and me, right from the start. To Heidi Stahl, who read the first draft and gave me extensive feedback, your suggestions and questions were invaluable and guided me time and again as I revised the work. And when I was finally ready, thank you John Runyan and Ann Spiers for reading the final copy. Your generous and encouraging responses gave me the confidence I needed to go to print. Thank you Nancy Morgan for your skillful and sensitive editing and Sy Novak for your support and creative genius. Thank you to Jeanie Okimoto and Endicott and Hugh Books for shepherding this book into print. Jeanie, you do so much to bring good stories into the world; you are an inspiration. I also wish to thank Mary Fitzgerald and Neva Dail Bridges for your steady friendship. You were always there even when I was not. And, to Becky Ernstes who, when I finally asked, you gave me your blessing. Your enduring friendship has never wavered and your blessing is a healing balm. I am also forever grateful to my parents who gave me life, supported my dreams, and encouraged me to write. And to Kate and Alex Rutherford, thank you for finding room in your hearts for me. The way you live your lives inspires me—every day. As I said in the book, "I cannot imagine my life without you." Finally, and most importantly, to Dana Illo, you are the love of my life. It was your love that opened my heart and your love that has sustained me these many years. You have given me so much: family, community, a life of beauty… and… five hundred miles across Spain. *Gracias, Gracias, Gracias.*

CPSIA information can be obtained
at www.ICGtesting.com
Printed in the USA
LVHW032331280120
645154LV00001B/115